P9-CMB-094

# THE RISE OF THE FIRST REICH

# MAJOR ISSUES IN HISTORY

Editor
C. WARREN HOLLISTER,
University of California, Santa Barbara

---

# THE RISE OF THE FIRST REICH

## Germany in the Tenth Century

*Boyd H. Hill, Jr.*

Department of History
University of Colorado

*John Wiley & Sons, Inc.*

New York • London • Sydney • Toronto

ST. PHILIPS COLLEGE LIBRARY

943,022
H655r

Copyright © 1969, by John Wiley & Sons, Inc.

All Rights reserved. No part of this book may be reproduced
by any means, nor transmitted, nor translated into a machine
language without the written permission of the publisher.

10 9 8 7 6 5 4 3 2 1

Library of Congress Catalog Card Number: 75-82977
Cloth: SNB 471 39611 7    Paper: SNB 471 39612 5
Printed in the United States of America

# SERIES PREFACE

The reading program in a history survey course traditionally has consisted of a large two-volume textbook and, perhaps, a book of readings. This simple reading program requires few decisions and little imagination on the instructor's part, and tends to encourage in the student the virtue of careful memorization. Such programs are by no means things of the past, but they certainly do not represent the wave of the future.

The reading program in survey courses at many colleges and universities today is far more complex. At the risk of over-simplification, and allowing for many exceptions and overlaps, it can be divided into four categories: (1) textbook, (2) original source readings, (3) specialized historical essays and interpretive studies, and (4) historical problems.

After obtaining an overview of the course subject matter (textbook), sampling the original sources, and being exposed to selective examples of excellent modern historical writing (historical essays), the student can turn to the crucial task of weighing various possible interpretations of major historical issues. It is at this point that memory gives way to creative critical thought. The "problems approach," in other words, is the intellectual climax of a thoughtfully conceived reading program and is, indeed, the most characteristic of all approaches to historical pedagogy among the newer generation of college and university teachers.

The historical problems books currently available are many and varied. Why add to this information explosion? Because the Wiley Major Issues Series constitutes an endeavor to produce something new that will respond to pedagogical needs thus far unmet. First, it is a series of individual volumes—one per problem. Many good teachers would much prefer to select their own historical issues rather than be tied to an inflexible sequence of issues imposed by a publisher and bound together between two

20826

covers. Second, the Wiley Major Issues Series is based on the idea of approaching the significant problems of history through a deft interweaving of primary sources and secondary analysis, fused together by the skill of a scholar-editor. It is felt that the essence of a historical issue cannot be satisfactorily probed either by placing a body of undigested source materials into the hands of inexperienced students or by limiting these students to the controversial literature of modern scholars who debate the meaning of sources the student never sees. This series approaches historical problems by exposing students to both the finest historical thinking on the issue and some of the evidence on which this thinking is based. This synthetic approach should prove far more fruitful than either the raw-source approach or the exclusively second-hand approach, for it combines the advantages—and avoids the serious disadvantages—of both.

Finally, the editors of the individual volumes in the Major Issues Series have been chosen from among the ablest scholars in their fields. Rather than faceless referees, they are historians who know their issues from the inside and, in most instances, have themselves contributed significantly to the relevant scholarly literature. It has been the editorial policy of this series to permit the editor-scholars of the individual volumes the widest possible latitude both in formulating their topics and in organizing their materials. Their scholarly competence has been unquestioningly respected; they have been encouraged to approach the problems as they see fit. The titles and themes of the series volumes have been suggested in nearly every case by the scholar-editors themselves. The criteria have been (1) that the issue be of relevance to undergraduate lecture courses in history, and (2) that it be an issue which the scholar-editor knows thoroughly and in which he has done creative work. And, in general, the second criterion has been given precedence over the first. In short, the question "What are the significant historical issues today?" has been answered not by general editors or sales departments but by the scholar-teachers who are responsible for these volumes.

*University of California,*                                    *C. Warren Hollister*
*Santa Barbara*

# ACKNOWLEDGMENTS

I wish to thank Mrs. Erika Koessler of the UCLA German Department and Mr. Rudolph Hirschmann, formerly with the German Department at the University of Colorado but now at the University of Rochester, for looking over some of my translations. These translations in many cases amount to a paraphrase of the original, and any errors are, of course, my own responsibility. I should also like to acknowledge a special debt to Professor Herwig Wolfram of the Institut für Österreichische Geschichtsforschung, Vienna, for his helpful comments on DO. III. 389.

# CONTENTS

# SECONDARY WORKS

# ART MONUMENTS

# Germany in the Tenth Century

DENMARK

NORTH SEA

Elbe

ENGLAND

FRIESLAND

WESTPHALIA

SAXONY

PHEAST

Bremen

Hildesheim

We

Gandersheim

Goslar

Corvey

Halbersta

THURING

Antwerp

LOWER

Cologne

Aachen

LORRAINE

Rhine

Fulda

WEST

EAS

Bamberg

Mainze

Forchhei

Trier

Worms

FRANCONIA

Reims

UPPER

Metz

Hirsau

Paris

LORRAINE

ALSACE

FRANCE

Augsburg

Lechfeld

SWABIA

Reichenau

St. Gall

Lech R.

UPPER

BURGUNDY

ITAL

Tre

LOWER

BURGUNDY

Milan

Pavia

# PROLOGUE

It was a hot summer day when the leader of the German army turned to address his men for the last time before going into battle against the attacking Hungarians.

"If the end lies near, my soldiers, it is better that we die gloriously in battle than be beaten by the enemy and then enslaved or strung up like animals." The demand for action required him to cut short his speech, and he finished his exhortation by saying, "Now let's open this conference with swords rather than with tongues." And so the legions of Otto I joined battle with the Hungarians at Lechfeld on August 10, 955.

Few battles in the history of Europe have been so important: it has even been called a "second Marathon." The stakes were high enough: the main question was whether Europe would continue to founder in the chaos that followed the disintegration of the Carolingian empire or whether the Continent would once again become a place of order.

The loyal troops of Otto carried the day. The Hungarians were routed and destroyed. In the Middle Ages, there was nothing so effective as a military victory to secure the throne and to make real the theoretical power of the monarch. Otto I could now resurrect the imperial claims of the Frankish emperor Charlemagne and create the first German Reich or empire. And the Germans could begin their march to the east and take up the double task of conquest and Christianization, a task inherited like so many others from Charlemagne.

The Ottonian empire would never rival the empire of a Trajan either in universality of thought or in geographical extent, much less in material wealth or in artistic creativity. But neither has any great power of modern times succeeded in rivalling the glories of ancient Rome. The success of the early German

1

ST. PHILIPS COLLEGE LIBRARY

kings and emperors in the tenth century laid the foundation for subsequent European developments, and it is the purpose of this collection to introduce the student to this important period in medieval history.

The selections have been chosen to illustrate the significance of tenth-century Germany and are aimed at the student whose background does not permit him to examine these sources in the original. This is not a work that purports to deal with tenth-century Europe or the concept of universal empire. However, since the empire was inextricably bound to the German nation, it is at times impossible to separate German history from imperial history.

What happened is this: the imperial concept was given a new lease on life on December 25, 800 when Charlemagne was crowned emperor in Rome. His son Louis the Pious maintained the empire but, following his death in 840, fragmentation, decentralization, and collapse quickly followed. Western Europe was divided into many petty kingdoms ruled by petty kinglets who found it difficult to withstand the combined attacks of the Vikings, the Hungarians, and the Saracens. The first part of the old Carolingian empire to recover was Germany (the Kingdom of the East Franks). Henry I, crowned king in 919, enjoyed some success, and this auspicious beginning was carried on by his son Otto, who became king in 936, defeated the Hungarians in 955, and marched into Italy to obtain the imperial crown in 962. The son and grandson of Otto carried on the tradition of their father in spite of the handicaps of short reigns and shorter lives, for Otto I ruled from 936 to 973, while his son Otto II enjoyed only a ten-year reign; and Otto III came to the throne at the age of three and died at 22 in 1002. To make a detailed comparison of the three monarchs would be unfair although some historians have been inclined to try. An impressionable and sensitive youth can hardly be compared to a seasoned veteran.

The first selection by Widukind of Corvey recounts the ceremony of royal coronation at Aachen in 936. This was a calculated affair in which the leaders of the realm symbolized their loyalty and devotion by waiting on their elected king at the banquet that followed the coronation ceremony. The second selection by Widukind is the narrative account of the battle of

Lechfeld, an event that was as important for European history as for the success of the Ottonian dynasty.

In "A Chronicle of Otto's Reign," Liudprand of Cremona provides us with insight into the diplomacy of the tenth century as well as with some shrewd observations about the papacy. His account of the troubles of Pope John is not only a good piece of narrative history, it also illuminates the relations between the government of Otto and the papacy and shows how the emperors so cavalierly overrode the natural ambitions of the Church. The second selection—Liudprand's droll and chauvinistic account of his trip to Constantinople—is justly famous. It gives us a remarkable case study of the struggle between east and west. The ambassador of the tenth century, just as of the twentieth, played the double role of spy and negotiator. The student should note the penetrating questions put to Liudprand by the emperor Nicephorus Phocas. In spite of his bombastic diatribe against the Byzantine empire, Liudprand's own critical acumen is demonstrated by his close observation of court life in Constantinople.

Within tenth-century Germany the study of Latin authors flourished, particularly at the nunnery of Gandersheim, an establishment that resembled an academy for noble young ladies more than a center of asceticism and mortification of the flesh. Here, intelligent girls devoted themselves to the study of Latin authors as well as to religious services. At Gandersheim, a particularly favored foundation of the ruling dynasty, Hroswitha composed poems, sang the praises of the emperor Otto, and wrote plays modeled on classical antecedents. Her play *Callimachus* is an illustration of virtue rewarded and vice punished through the intercession of St. John but, although the theme is purely Christian, the form shows more classical influence than that of any other playwright for several centuries before or after. Thus, Hroswitha's drama is an unprecedented link in the history of the theater as well as a sign of the artistic sophistication of tenth-century Germany.

Francis Tschan's exhaustive study of Bernward of Hildesheim gives a narrative account of one of the great church administrators and artistic patrons who served the Saxon dynasty. "In the Service of Otto III" tells the story of Bernward's arrival in Rome in January, 1001, and of meeting the emperor, his former pupil. Bernward had come to press his claim over the boundaries of Hildesheim and, while visiting Rome, he participated in the siege of Tivoli, an example of Bernward's steadfast loyalty to his emperor. The pacification of Tivoli was followed by rebellious rumblings on the part of the Romans, and in this selection is Otto's address to the citizens of Rome about their obligations and duties to their emperor. The speech comes to us through Thangmar, Bernward's confidant who accompanied him on the journey.

In the same year that Bernward visited Rome, Leo of Vercelli, Otto's chancellor, issued in the name of the emperor a deed granting eight counties to the Roman Church (DO. III. 389). The most remarkable feature of the document is its explicit statement that the Donation of Constantine is a patent forgery, a fact that had to be rediscovered in the fifteenth century by Lorenzo Valla.

The recipient of DO. III. 389 was Gerbert of Aurillac (Pope Sylvester II), tutor and friend of the emperor as well as ruler of the Church. Gerbert's intellectual prowess, based on his success as a scholar and teacher and particularly on his popularization of Indic-Arabic numerals, made him a legend in his own time. He was considered something of a magician to later generations. Carl Jung observes in *Psyche and Symbol* (p. 189) that Gerbert was commonly thought to have possessed an oracular golden head, which assisted him in his endeavors. However, Lynn Thorndike in *A History of Magic and Experimental Science* (I, 705) says that the head did not always give the correct answers to the problems put to it! Such legends were commonly attributed to men of science in the Middle Ages, a time when the line between science and magic was not so arbitrarily drawn as it is today. The selection given here, however, shows Gerbert as chief ideologist of the empire under Otto III. As Pope Sylvester II, he was in a strong position to aid his master in the attempt to recreate the forms if not the substance of the ancient Roman government.

The second section of this work is a series of essays written by modern historians. These selections in many cases bear directly on the literary and artistic documents of the Ottonian period, for example, Percy Schramm's study of DO. III. 389 and the iconographical study of Ernest Kantorowicz which treats the imperial miniature found in the Aachen Gospels. The articles of Geoffrey Barraclough and Walter Ullmann deal with the constitutional foundations and the ecclesiastical relations of the empire. Carl Erdmann's study concerns itself with the growth of the idea of *imperium,* a word that originally meant the right to command but which has a much broader meaning in the Middle Ages, principally the dominion and rule of the emperor as well as the empire itself. Sometimes the word *imperium* has several connotations and, for this reason, it is left untranslated. Martin Lintzel gives a balanced critique of Otto I's imperial policy and logically demonstrates that both the extreme champions and the severest critics of Otto's rule can learn more from the tenth century than they can from applying later examples of imperial policy to an earlier age.

The selected art monuments illustrated in *The Rise of the First Reich* are not meant to be a kind of refreshing pause from the study of the documents but are themselves some of our most important remains of the tenth century. To say simply that a monarch was both priest and king or that an emperor possessed divine attributes is pale and vapid when compared to the sight of the emperor in the Aachen Gospels (Plate 14): he sits on a throne with his feet resting on Mother Earth and his head in the heavens, just as Christ in Majesty is depicted. At a time when there are gaps in written sources, the political or intellectual historian must consider the art works themselves for an understanding of the First Reich. The student should not be misled by the relative crudeness of Ottonian art when compared with earlier classical art or later Gothic. It has been said of the Hildesheim Doors that they are "dynamically alive, instinct with a vigor that seems almost to tear them free of their relief backing." And of the expulsion panel, the same authors say:

"The *Judgment of Adam and Eve* is rendered with the naive sense of the dramatic that makes the observer forget the crudely shaped bodies with their overlarge heads and unarticulated limbs. The unknown sculptor's power of characterization transcends his lack of anatomical knowledge . . . the sense of movement arising from the sheer vitality of the figures themselves unites them in common submission to some unseen but irresistible power."[1]

[1] David M. Robb and J. J. Garrison, *Art in the Western World* (New York: Harper & Brothers, 1935), pp. 474–475.

## CHRONOLOGICAL TABLE OF THE TENTH CENTURY

| | |
|---|---|
| 919–936 | King Henry I, the Fowler |
| 924 | Hungarians besiege the castle of Werla near the Harz mountains |
| 926 | Rudolf II of Upper Burgundy hands over the Holy Lance to Henry I in Worms |
| 929 | Marriage of Henry's son Otto to Princess Edith of England |
| 933 | Victory of the Germans over the Hungarians at Riade on the river Unstrut, near Merseburg |
| 936 | Death of Henry I and burial at Quedlinburg |
| 936–973 | Otto I, the Great |
| c. 935–1000 | Hroswitha, nun and poet of Gandersheim |
| c. 940 | Widukind enters the monastery of Corvey |
| 946 | Death of Queen Edith |
| 950–962 | Rule of King Berengar II and his son Adalbert over Italy |
| 951 | Otto's first Italian campaign and his marriage to Adelaide, widow of King Lothair II of Italy |
| 955 | Battle of Lechfeld |
| 961–964 | Otto's second Italian campaign |
| 962 | Imperial coronation of Otto I in Rome by Pope John XII |
| | Liutprand is made bishop of Cremona by Otto |
| 963 | Otto has Pope John XII deposed and replaced by Leo VIII |
| 967 | Widukind begins his *History of the Saxons* |
| 968 | Liutprand of Cremona goes to Constantinople as Otto's ambassador |
| 968 | Completion of Hroswitha's poem *The Deeds of Otto* |
| 972 | Marriage of Otto II and the Byzantine princess Theophano |

| | |
|---|---|
| 973 | Death of Otto the Great in Memleben and burial in the cathedral at Magdeburg |
| 973–983 | Emperor Otto II |
| 980–982 | Otto II invades Italy and is defeated by the Saracens in Calabria |
| 983 | Death of Otto II and burial in Rome |
| 983–1002 | Emperor Otto III |
| 991 | Death of Empress Theophano and assumption of Otto's guardianship by his grandmother Adelaide |
| 993–1022 | Bernward, bishop of Hildesheim |
| 996 | Otto III crowned in Rome by Pope Gregory V |
| 999 | Gerbert of Aurillac becomes Pope Sylvester II |
| 1000 | Hungarians accept Christianity |
| 1001 | Uprising in Rome |
| | Bishop Bernward lays the first stone of St. Michael's Church in Hildesheim |
| 1002 | Death of Otto III and burial at the cathedral in Aachen |
| 1002–1024 | Emperor Henry II |
| 1003 | Death of Pope Sylvester II |
| 1009–1018 | Thietmar, bishop of Merseburg |
| 1014 | Imperial coronation of Henry II at Rome by Pope Benedict VIII |
| c. 1015 | Bronze doors and column of Bishop Bernward of Hildesheim |

PARTIAL GENEALOGICAL CHART
OF THE SAXON DYNASTY


Liudolf, d. 866
Duke of Saxony
m. Oda

Otto, d. 912
Duke of Saxony
m. Hadwig

*Henry I*, the Fowler
919–936
m. Mathilda

Henry, d. 955 —————— *Otto I*, the Great —————— Bruno, d. 965
Duke of                    936–973                   Archbishop of
Bavaria                    m. Edith of England 929   Cologne,
m. Judith,                 m. Adelaide of Lombardy 951  Duke of
daughter of                                          Lotharingia
Duke Arnulf
of Bavaria

*Otto II*
973–983
m. Theophano 973

Henry the Wrangler        *Otto III*
d. 995                    983–1002
Duke of Bavaria
m. Gisela of Burgundy

*Henry II*
1002–1024
m. Kunigunde

# SOURCES

# 1     *Widukind of Corvey*

*Widukind, author of the* Res gestae Saxonicae *(History of the Saxons), was born about 925 and probably entered the Benedictine monastery of Corvey in 940. Few other facts are known about him, including his death date, but he remains the principal source for the events of Otto's life. Of the two selections below, the first concerns the royal coronation of 936, an important source for the history of coronations in general. The second selection tells of Otto's victory over the Hungarians at the Battle of Lechfeld in 955, which R. W. Southern in the* Making of the Middle Ages *compares to the battle of Marathon.*

*See Plates 1 and 2—the Abbey Church at Corvey—and Plate 3—a page of the Widukind manuscript in the British Museum.*

---

## THE CORONATION OF OTTO I

After the death of Henry [919–936], the father of his country and greatest and best of all kings, the Franks and Saxons chose as their prince his son Otto, who had already been designated king by his father. They ordered the coronation to be held at the palace in Aachen—the place of universal election. . . .

And when they had arrived, the dukes and the great lords

SOURCE. *Widukindi monachi Corbeiensis Rerum gestarum Saxonicarum Libri tres*, ed. G. Waitz et al., 5th ed. (*Scriptores rerum Germanicarum in usu scholarum ex monumentis Germaniae separatim editi* [Hannover: Hahnsche Buchhandlung, 1935]), pp. 63–67; trans. Boyd H. Hill, Jr.

9

PLATE I. Exterior of the westwork of the Abbey Church at Corvey
c. 870 (Marburg—Art Reference Bureau).

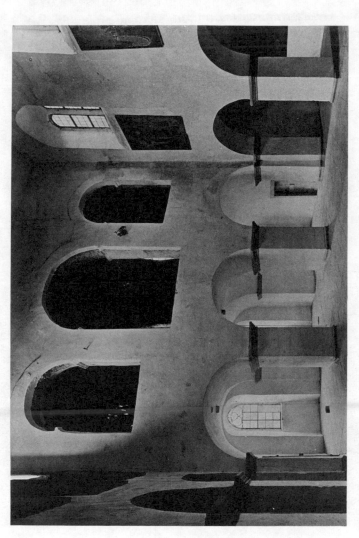

PLATE II. Interior of the westwork of the Abbey Church at Corvey (Marburg—Art Reference Bureau).

11

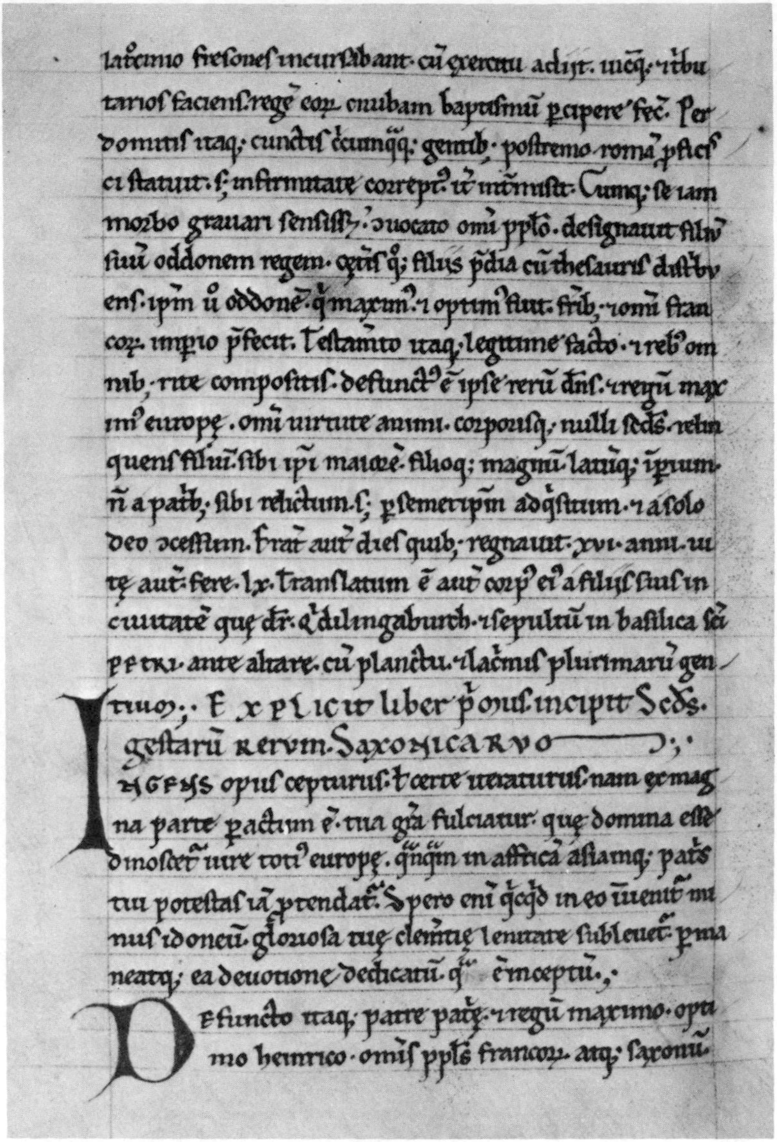

PLATE III. Widukind Manuscript (London, British Museum, Add. MS. 22109, twelfth century, fol. 155ᵛ).

with a force of the chief vassals gathered in the portico of the basilica of Charlemagne. They placed the new ruler on the throne that had been constructed there, giving him their hands and offering fealty; promising their help against all his enemies, they made him king according to their custom.

While this part of the ceremony was being carried out by the dukes and other magistrates, Archbishop Hildibert of Mainz [927–937] awaited the procession of the new king with all the priestly order and the commoners in the basilica. The archbishop awaited the procession of the king, holding the crozier in his right hand and wearing the alb, the pallium, and the chasuble. When the king came forward, he advanced to meet him, touching the king's right hand with his left. Then he led the king to the middle of the sanctuary and turned to the people standing about them (ambulatories had been constructed above and below in that round basilica so that all the people might have a good view).

"Lo," Hildibert said, "I bring before you Lord Otto elected by God, formerly designated by Henry, now made king by all the princes. If this election pleases you, signify by raising your right hand to heaven." To this all the people raising their right hands on high loudly called down prosperity on the new ruler.

The king, dressed in a close-fitting tunic according to Frankish custom, was escorted behind the altar, on which lay the royal insignia—sword with sword-belt, cloak with bracelets, staff with scepter and diadem.

Archbishop Hildibert, the highest bishop at this time, was a Frank by race, a monk by profession, brought up and educated in the monastery of Fulda. Because of his superior ability he was made abbot of Fulda after which he attained the most exalted rank—that of the archbishop of Mainz. He was a man of wonderful sanctity and superior intellect.

Among other divine gifts he was said to possess the ability to prophesy. When the question of who should crown the king arose, two bishops besides Hildibert were considered eligible: the bishop of Trier because his city was the most ancient and had been founded by St. Peter, and the bishop of Cologne because the place of coronation—Aachen—was in his diocese. But both of these men who would have enjoyed the honor deferred to the preeminence of Archbishop Hildibert.

Going to the altar and taking from it the sword with sword-belt and turning to the king, he said:

"Accept this sword, with which you may chase out all the adversaries of Christ, barbarians and bad Christians, by the divine authority handed down to you and by the power of all the empire of the Franks, for the most lasting peace of all Christians."

Then taking the bracelets and cloak, he clothed him saying, "These points [of the cloak] falling to ground will remind you with what zeal of faith you should burn and how you ought to endure in preserving peace to the end."

Then taking the scepter and staff, he said: "With these symbols you may be reminded that you should reproach your subjects with paternal castigation, but first of all you should extend the hand of mercy to ministers of God, widows, and orphans. And never let the oil of compassion be absent from your head in order that you may be crowned with eternal reward in the present and in the future."

After having been sprinkled with holy oil and crowned with a golden diadem by the bishops Hildibert and Wikfried [of Cologne, 924–953] and all legal consecration having been completed, the king was led to the throne, to which he ascended by means of a spiral staircase. The throne of marvelous beauty had been constructed between two marble pillars, and from there the king could see and be seen by all.

After the divine praise was intoned and the mass was solemnly celebrated, the king descended from the throne and walked to the palace. Going up to a marble table decorated with regal utensils, he sat down with the bishops and all the people while the dukes waited on them.

Gilbert, Duke of the Lotharingians [915–939], in whose district Aachen lay, made all the arrangements. Eberhard [Duke of Franconia, 918–939] presided over the table. Herman the Frank [Duke of Swabia, 926–949] supervised the cupbearers; Arnulf [Duke of Bavaria, 907–937] oversaw the order of knights and the choice of the camp site. Count Siegfried [d. 937], highest of the Saxons next to the king and brother-in-law of the former king [Henry I], administered Saxony during this time against enemy attack, and he also took care of the young Henry [Otto's brother and Duke of Bavaria, 947–955].

The king, after honoring each of the great lords according to regal munificence by an appropriate gift, dismissed the multitude with great good cheer.


## THE BATTLE OF LECHFELD[1]

Having returned to Saxony around the Kalends of July Otto met Hungarian legates who were apparently visiting him on account of ancient fealty and favor. In fact, however, it seemed to some that they had come in order to ascertain the outcome of the civil war [in Bavaria].

They stayed with him for some days, and he dismissed them in peace after having parceled out some small gifts. Subsequently he heard from messengers sent by his brother [Henry], the Duke of the Bavarians: "The Hungarians have spread out and invaded your territory; they are determined to go to war with you." When the king heard this, he advanced to meet the enemy undaunted by the previous conflict. Only a very few of the Saxons were with him because he had been pressing for a war against the Slavs. When the camp had been set up within the city of Augsburg, an army of Franks and Bavarians came to his aid. Duke Conrad [the Red, former duke of Lotharingia] also hurried to the camp with a strong force of cavalry; his arrival encouraged the soldiers, who now did not wish to delay battle. Conrad was dear to his companions both at home and in the field, for he was by nature bold of mind and what is rare in the brave, he was also a man of good judgment. Whenever he ran against the enemy as a horseman or a foot-soldier, he was an irresistible warrior.

Scouting forces of both sides ascertained that the two armies were not far distant from each other. Otto's forces were ordered to fast and to be ready for war on the next day [10 August 955]. At the first rays of dawn the troops received and accepted the protection of their commander and then promised him their

---

[1] *Res gestae Saxonicae*, ed. Waitz, pp. 123–129.

service. And after they had sworn an oath to one another, they raised their standards and proceeded from camp, about eight legions in all. [A legion consisted of at least 1,000 men.]

The army was led through rugged terrain so that the enemy would not have an opportunity to shoot arrows at them. The Bavarians formed the first, second, and third legions, which Duke Henry's subordinates were in charge of, for the dying Henry [d. Nov. 1, 955] was absent as a result of the last campaign. The Franks constituted the fourth legion, under the command of Duke Conrad.

In the fifth and largest legion, called the "royal," was the prince himself in the midst of a thousand hand-picked youthful soldiers, and before him the victorious Archangel [Michael], thickly surrounded by troops. The Swabians made up the sixth and seventh legions; they were commanded by Burchard, whom the king's brother's daughter had married.[2] In the eighth were the Bohemians, a thousand strong, whose expertise was supply. They were in last place, presumably the safest.

But events turned out otherwise than expected, for the Hungarians did not delay at all but crossed the river Lech and surrounded the army while harassing the last legion with arrows. With a loud shout they attacked, killed or captured most of the eighth legion, and having taken possession of the baggage, they compelled the other soldiers of that legion to flee.

Similarly they attacked the seventh and sixth legions and put many of them to flight. When the king discovered that the battle was still ahead of him and that the rear columns were already in danger, he sent Duke Conrad back with the fourth legion, who pulled out the captives, cast out the booty, and drove the plundering columns of the enemy forward. The enemy were surrounded on all sides, and Duke Conrad returned to the king with the standards of victory. It is somewhat strange that veteran soldiers who were accustomed to the glory of victory had delayed fighting, whereas Duke Conrad held a triumph with troops who were new and virtually ignorant of waging war. . . .

When the king saw that the whole burden of the fight was

---

[2] Burchard III, Duke of Swabia (954–973), married Hedwig, daughter of Henry, Duke of Bavaria (947–955), who was a brother of Otto I.

now in front he spoke in order to encourage his comrades. "It is up to us good men in this emergency, as you yourselves see, my soldiers, not to tolerate the enemy at a distance but only face to face. For up to now I have made glorious use of your energetic hands and unconquerable weapons everywhere outside my own soil and *imperium*. Shall I now turn my back on my land and realm? We are surpassed, I know, by numbers, but not by courage or arms. For we know that for the most part they are devoid of all armor, and what is a greater solace to us, they are deprived of the help of God. Their audacity is like a wall of defense, but we have the hope of divine protection.

"Now it would shame almost all the rulers of Europe to give in to the enemy. If the end lies near, my soldiers, it is better that we die gloriously in battle than be beaten by the enemy and enslaved or strung up like animals. I would say more, my soldiers, if I could augment your courage or boldness by words. Now let's open this conference with swords rather than with tongues."

And when he had finished speaking, he seized his shield and the Holy Lance, and being the first to turn his horse to the enemy he was a most valiant warrior and excellent commander.[3]

[3] The Holy Lance, which supposedly contained in its shaft one of the nails of the Cross of Christ, became a symbol of rule among the Germans. As early as the first century A.D. we learn from Tacitus that German youths were presented with a lance, at which time they became full-fledged members of the tribe (*Germania*, chap. 13). By the eighth century the lance had been combined with the battle standard, and we find Charlemagne represented on his official seal with crown, shield, and lance. The Lombards used the lance as a symbol at the royal coronation (last seen in 735 at the elevation of King Hildebrand). On the Bayeux tapestry William the Conqueror is shown receiving the ambassadors of Harold Godwinson (d. 1066), who is distinguished from the others by the possession of a banner-lance. The lance retained its symbolic royal worth until the end of the tenth century when it was replaced by the throne, the crown, and the scepter. It was a great coup for Henry the Fowler when he received the Holy Lance in 926 from Rudolf II of Burgundy (912–937) in exchange for a piece of property east of the river Aar. (The Aargau today lies immediately west of Zurich.) According to Liudprand Otto I knelt down by the lance before the battle of Birten in 939 and won the fight. Although the history of the lance is obscure and may well have been influenced by the traditions both of pagan Germans and of classical Romans as well as by Christian legends, there is no doubt that it had a central

At first the bolder of the enemy resisted, but then as they saw their companions being routed, and stunned at being surrounded by us, they were ultimately killed.

Some of those remaining whose horses were tired out entered nearby villages, and being surrounded by soldiers were burned up along with the buildings. Others swam the nearby river, and when they could not get a foothold on the farther bank, they were swallowed up by the river and perished. On that day the [Hungarian] camp was invaded and all the captives were set free. On the second and third day the remaining Hungarians from the neighboring cities were virtually annihilated so that hardly any of them got away; but the victory over such a cruel tribe was not of course won without bloodshed to our side.

Duke Conrad was fighting hard, and on fire with purpose and with the heat of the sun, which was oppressive that day, he loosened the bonds of his cuirass to take a breath of air and was killed by an arrow in the throat. On the king's command his body was picked up and honorably transported to Worms. This man, famous for greatness of mind and body, was interred there with the weeping and wailing of all Franks.

Three leaders of the Hungarians were captured, and being presented to Duke Henry they died as they deserved by hanging.

The king having been made glorious by his army was hailed as father of his country and *Imperator*[4] in a celebrated triumph. Then he decreed that God and His Holy Mother be honored and praised in every church. Amidst dancing and joy he returned victorious to Saxony and was lovingly received by his people, for such a great royal victory had not been celebrated in the 200 years before the reign of Otto.

---

place among royal insignia during the Ottonian period. See Percy Ernst Schramm, "Die 'Heilige Lanze,' " in *Herrschaftszeichen und Staatssymbolik*, 3 vols. (Stuttgart: Hiersemann Verlag, 1954-56), II, pp. 492-537, and Laura Hibbard Loomis, "The Holy Relics of Charlemagne and King Athelstan: The Lances of Longinus and St. Mauricius," *Speculum*, XXV (1950), pp. 440-456.

[4] *Imperator* means both victorious field commander and emperor.

# 2        *Liudprand of Cremona*

*Liudprand (or Liutprand) was born in A.D. 920 at Pavia, grew up in a wealthy Lombard family, and left Italy to join Otto's court in 956. He knew Latin, Greek, and German. In 960 he went to Constantinople on a mission for Otto and was given the bishopric of Cremona at the end of 961. From this time on he remained a loyal member of Otto's diplomatic service. He made another journey to Constantinople in June, 968, to arrange a marriage between the Emperor's son Otto II and the Princess Theophano. The wedding ultimately took place in Rome in 972. Older works (including Wright's translation of Liudprand) considered Theophano the daughter of Emperor Romanus II (959–963), but recent authorities generally agree that she was the niece of John Tzimisces, who followed Nicephorus Phocas as Byzantine emperor. (See* Cambridge Mediaeval History, *IV [1966], 163, n. 1.) Liudprand died in January 972, a year before the death of Otto I.*

---

## A CHRONICLE OF OTTO'S REIGN

Berengar [of Ivrea, King of Italy, 950–961] and Adalbert [Berengar's son, and co-King of Italy, 950–961] were reigning, or rather raging, in Italy, where to speak the truth they exercised the worst of tyrannies, when John [XII, 955–964], the supreme pontiff and universal pope, whose church had suffered from the savage cruelty of the aforesaid Berengar and Adalbert, sent envoys from the Holy Church of Rome, in the persons of the Cardinal Deacon John and the [papal] secretary Azo, to Otto, at that time the most serene and pious king and now our august emperor, humbly begging him both by letters and a recital of facts for the love of God and the Holy Apostles Peter and Paul,

SOURCE. Liudprand of Cremona, "A Chronicle of Otto's Reign," *The Works of Liudprand of Cremona,* trans. F. A. Wright (London: Routledge & Kegan Paul, Ltd., 1930), pp. 215–218. Reprinted by permission of Routledge & Kegan Paul, Ltd.

whom he hoped would remit his sins, to rescue him and the Holy Roman Church entrusted to him from their jaws, and restore it to its former prosperity and freedom.

While the Roman envoys were laying these complaints, Waldpert, the venerable archbishop of the holy church of Milan, having escaped half dead from the mad rage of the aforesaid Berengar and Adalbert, sought the powerful protection of the above-mentioned Otto, at that time king and now our august emperor, declaring that he could no longer bear or submit to the cruelty of Berengar and Adalbert and Willa [Berengar's wife], who contrary to all human and divine law had appointed Manasses Bishop of Arles to the see of Milan. He said that it was a calamity for his church thus to intercept a right that belonged to him and to his people. After Waldpert came Waldo Bishop of Como, crying out that he also had suffered a like insult at the hands of Berengar, Adalbert, and Willa. With the apostolic envoys there also arrived some members of the laity, among them the illustrious marquess Otbert [of the House of Este, died c. 974], asking help and advice from his most sacred majesty Otto, then king now emperor.

The most pious king was moved by their tearful complaints, and considered not himself but the cause of Jesus Christ. Therefore, although it was contrary to custom, he appointed his young son Otto as king, and leaving him in Saxony collected his forces and marched in haste to Italy [August, 961]. There he drove Berengar and Adalbert from the realm at once, the more quickly inasmuch as it is certain that the Holy Apostles Peter and Paul were fighting under his flag. The good king brought together what had been scattered and mended what had been broken, restoring to each man his due possessions. Then he advanced on Rome to do the same again.

There he was welcomed with marvelous ceremony and unexampled pomp, and was anointed as emperor by John the supreme bishop and universal pope [February 2, 962]. To the Church he not only gave back her possessions but bestowed lavish gifts of jewels, gold, and silver. Furthermore, Pope John and all the princes of the city swore solemnly on the most precious body of Saint Peter that they would never give help to Berengar and Adalbert. Thereupon Otto returned to Pavia with all speed.

Meanwhile Pope John, forgetful of his oath and the promise he had made to the sacred emperor, sent to Adalbert asking him to return and swearing that he would assist him against the power of the most sacred emperor. For the sacred emperor had so terrified this Adalbert, persecutor of God's churches and of Pope John, that he had left Italy altogether and had gone to Fraxinetum and put himself under the protection of the Saracens.[1] The righteous emperor for his part could not understand at all why Pope John was now showing such affection to the very man whom previously he had attacked in bitter hatred. Accordingly he called together some of his intimates and sent off to Rome to inquire if this report was true. On his messengers' arrival they got this answer, not from a few chance informants, but from all the citizens of Rome:

"Pope John hates the most sacred emperor, who freed him from Adalbert's clutches, for exactly the same reason that the devil hates his creator. The emperor, as we have learned by experience, knows, works, and loves the things of God: he guards the affairs of church and state with his sword, adorns them by his virtues, and purifies them by his laws. Pope John is the enemy of all these things. What we say is a tale well known to all. As witness to its truth take the widow of Rainer his own vassal, a woman with whom John has been so blindly in love that he has made her governor of many cities and given to her the golden crosses and cups that are the sacred possessions of St. Peter himself.

"Witness also the case of Stephana, his father's mistress, who recently conceived a child by him and died of an effusion of blood.[2] If all else were silent, the palace of the Lateran, that once sheltered saints and is now a harlot's brothel, will never forget his union with his father's wench, the sister of the other concubine Stephania.

[1] Fraxinetum or Le Frainet was on the Côte d'Azur midway between Marseilles and Nice.

[2] John's father was Alberic II of Spoleto, Prince of Rome (932–954).

"Witness again the absence of all women here save Romans: they fear to come and pray at the thresholds of the Holy Apostles, for they have heard how John a little time ago took women pilgrims by force to his bed—wives, widows, and virgins alike.

"Witness the churches of the Holy Apostles, whose roof lets the rain in upon the sacrosanct altar, and that not in drops but in sheets. The woodwork fills us with alarm, when we go there to ask God's help. Death reigns within the building, and though we have much to pray for, we are prevented from going there and soon shall be forced to abandon God's house altogether.

"Witness the women he keeps, some of them fine ladies, who as the poet [Terence] says are as thin as reeds by dieting, others everyday buxom wenches. It is all the same to him whether they walk the pavement or ride in a carriage and pair [Juvenal]. That is the reason why there is the same disagreement between him and the holy emperor as there is of necessity between wolves and lambs [Horace]. That he may go his way unchecked, he is trying to get Adalbert as patron, guardian, and protector."

When the envoys on their return gave this report to the Emperor, he said: "He is only a boy, and will soon alter if good men set him an example. I hope that honorable reproof and generous persuasion will quickly cure him of these vices, and then we shall say with the prophet, 'This is a change which the hand of the Highest has brought.'" He added: "The first thing required by circumstances is that we dislodge Berengar from his position on Montefeltro. Then let us address some words of fatherly admonition to the Lord Pope. His sense of shame, if not his own wishes, will soon effect a change in him for the better. Perchance if he is forced into good ways, he will be ashamed to get out of them again."

## THE EMBASSY TO CONSTANTINOPLE[3]

On the sixth of June [968], which was the Saturday before Pentecost, I was brought before the Emperor's brother Leo,

[3] Liudprand of Cremona, "The Embassy to Constantinople," *The Works of Liudprand of Cremona*, trans F. A. Wright, (London: Routledge & Kegan Paul Ltd., 1930) pp. 236–245. Reprinted by permission of the publisher.

marshal of the court and chancellor; and there we tired ourselves with a fierce argument over your imperial title. He called
you not Emperor, which is Basileus in his tongue [Greek], but
insultingly Rex, which is King in ours. I told him that the thing
meant was the same though the word was different, and he then
said that I had come not to make peace but to stir up strife.
Finally he got up in a rage, and really wishing to insult us
received your letter not in his own hand but through an inter-
preter. He is a man commanding enough in person but feigning
humility: whereon if a man lean it will pierce his hand.

On the seventh of June, the sacred day of Pentecost, I was
brought before Nicephorus [Phocas] himself [963–969] in the
palace called Stephana, that is, the Crown Palace. He is a mon-
strosity of a man, a dwarf, fat-headed and with tiny mole's eyes;
disfigured by a short, broad, thick beard half going gray; dis-
graced by a neck scarcely an inch long; piglike by reason of the
big close bristles on his head; in color an Ethiopian and as
the poet [Juvenal] says, "you would not like to meet him in the
dark"; a big belly, a lean posterior, very long in the hip considering his short stature, small legs, fair-sized heels and feet;
dressed in a robe made of fine linen, but old, foul-smelling, and
discolored by age; shod with Sicyonian slippers;[4] bold of tongue,
a fox by nature, in perjury and falsehood a Ulysses. My Lords
and August Emperors, you always seemed comely to me, but
how much more comely now! Always magnificent, how much
more magnificent now! Always mighty, how much more mighty
now! Always clement, how much more clement now! Always
full of virtues, how much fuller now! At his left, not on a line
with him, but much lower down, sat the two child emperors,
once his masters, now his subjects. He began his speech as
follows:

"It was our duty and our desire to give you a courteous and
magnificent reception. That, however, has been rendered impossible by the impiety of your master, who in the guise of an
hostile invader has laid claim to Rome; has robbed Berengar and
Adalbert of their kingdom contrary to law and right; has slain

---

[4] Sicyon or Secyon was an ancient Greek city of the northern Pelopon-
nesus noted for painting and sculpture in bronze.

some of the Romans by the sword, some by hanging, while others he had either blinded or sent into exile; and furthermore has tried to subdue to himself by massacre and conflagration cities belonging to our empire. His wicked attempts have proved unsuccessful, and so he has sent you, the instigator and furtherer of this villainy, under pretence of peace to act *comme un espion*, that is, as a spy upon us.[5]

To him I made this reply: "My master did not invade the city of Rome by force nor as a tyrant; he freed her from a tyrant's yoke, or rather from the yoke of many tyrants. Was she not ruled by effeminate debauchers, and what is even worse and more shameful, by harlots? Your power, methinks, was fast asleep then; and the power of your predecessors, who in name alone are called emperors of the Romans, while the reality is far different. If they were powerful, if they were emperors of the Romans, why did they allow Rome to be in the hands of harlots? Were not some of the holy popes banished, others so distressed that they could not procure their daily supplies nor money wherewith to give alms? Did not Adalbert send insulting letters to your predecessors, the emperors Romanos [II, 959–963] and Constantine [VII, 913–959]? Did he not rob and plunder the churches of the Holy Apostles? Who of you emperors, led by zeal for God, troubled to punish so heinous a crime and bring back the Holy Church to its proper state? You neglected it, my master did not. From the ends of the world he rose, and came to Rome, and drove out the ungodly, and gave back to the vicars of the Holy Apostles all their power and honor. Those who afterwards rose against him and the Lord Pope, as being violators of their oath, sacrilegious robbers and torturers of their lords the popes, in accordance with the decrees of such Roman emperors as Justinian, Valentinian, Theodosius etc., he slew, beheaded, hanged or exiled. If he had not done so, he himself would be an impious, unjust, cruel tyrant. It is a known fact that Berengar and Adalbert became his vassals and received the kingdom of Italy with a golden sceptre from his hand and that they promised fealty under oath in the presence of your servants, men still alive and now dwelling in this city. At the devil's prompting

---

[5] The translator uses French where Liudprand used Greek.

they perfidiously broke their word, and therefore he justly took their kingdom from them, as being deserters and rebels. You yourself would have done the same to men who had sworn fealty and then revolted against you."

"But," said he, "there is one of Adalbert's vassals here, and he does not acknowledge the truth of this."

"If he denies it," I replied, "one of my men, at your command, will prove to him tomorrow in single combat that it is so."

"Well," said he, "he may, as you declare, have acted justly in this. Explain now why he attacked the borders of our empire with war and conflagration. We were friends and were thinking by marriage to enter into a partnership that would never be broken."

"The land," I answered, "which you say belongs to your empire, is proved by race and language to be part of the kingdom of Italy. The Lombards held it in their power, and Louis, emperor of the Lombards or Franks, freed it from the grip of the Saracens with great slaughter.[6] For seven years [c. 927–934] also Landulf, prince of Benevento and Capua, held it under his control. Nor would it even now have passed from the yoke of slavery to him and his descendants, had not your emperor Romanos bought at a great price the friendship of our king Hugh.[7] It was for this reason also that he made a match between king Hugh's bastard daughter and his own nephew and namesake. I see now that you think it shows weakness in my master, not generosity, when after winning Italy and Rome he for so many years left them to you. The friendly partnership, which you say you wished to form by a marriage, we hold to be a fraud and a snare: you ask for a truce, but you have no real reason to want it nor we to grant it. Come, let us clear away all trickeries and speak the plain truth. My master has sent me to you to see if you will give the daughter of the emperor Romanos and the empress Theophano to his son, my master the august emperor Otto. If you give me your oath that the marriage shall take place, I am to affirm to you under oath that my master in grateful return will observe to do this and this for you. Moreover he has already given you, his

[6] Louis II, d. 875.
[7] Hugh of Arles, King of Italy, 926–948.

brother ruler, the best pledge of friendship by handing over Apulia, which was subject to his rule. I, to whose suggestion you declare this mischief was due, intervened in this matter, and there are as many witnesses to this as there are people in Apulia."

"It is past seven o'clock," said Nicephorus "and there is a church procession which I must attend. Let us keep to the business before us. We will give you a reply at some convenient season."

I think that I shall have as much pleasure in describing this procession as my masters will have in reading of it. A numerous company of tradesmen and low-born persons, collected on this solemn occasion to welcome and honour Nicephorus, lined the sides of the road, like walls, from the palace to Saint Sophia, tricked out with thin little shields and cheap spears. As an additional scandal, most of the mob assembled in his honor had marched there with bare feet, thinking, I suppose, that thus they would better adorn the sacred procession. His nobles for their part, who with their master passed through the plebeian and barefoot multitude, were dressed in tunics that were too large for them and were also because of their extreme age full of holes. They would have looked better if they had worn their ordinary clothes. There was not a man among them whose grandfather had owned his tunic when it was new. No one except Nicephorus wore any jewels or golden ornaments, and the emperor looked more disgusting than ever in the regalia that had been designed to suit the persons of his ancestors. By your life, sires, dearer to me than my own, one of your nobles' costly robes is worth a hundred or more of these. I was taken to the procession and given a place on a platform near the singers.

As Nicephorus, like some crawling monster, walked along, the singers began to cry out in adulation: "Behold the morning star approaches: the day star rises: in his eyes the sun's rays are reflected: Nicephorus our prince, the pale death of the Saracens." And then they cried again: "Long life, long life to our prince Nicephorus. Adore him, ye nations, worship him, bow the neck to his greatness." How much more truly might they have sung: "Come, you miserable burnt-out coal; old woman in your walk, wood-devil in your look; clod-hopper, haunter of byres, goat-footed, horned, double-limbed; bristly, wild, rough, barbarian, harsh, hairy, a rebel, a Cappadocian!" So, puffed up by these lying ditties, he entered St. Sophia, his masters the emperors following at a distance and doing him homage on the ground with the kiss of peace. His armour bearer, with an arrow for pen, recorded in the church the era in progress since the beginning of his reign. So those who did not see the ceremony know what era it is.

On this same day he ordered me to be his guest. But as he did not think me worthy to be placed above any of his nobles, I sat fifteenth from him and without a table cloth. Not only did no one of my suite sit at table with me; they did not even set eyes upon the house where I was entertained. At the dinner which was fairly foul and disgusting, washed down with oil after the fashion of drunkards and moistened also with an exceedingly bad fish liquor, the emperor asked me many questions concerning your power, your dominions and your army. My answers were sober and truthful; but he shouted out: "You lie. Your master's soldiers cannot ride and they do not know how to fight on foot. The size of their shields, the weight of their cuirasses, the length of their swords, and the heaviness of their helmets, does not allow them to fight either way." Then with a smile he added: "Their gluttony also prevents them. Their God is their belly, their courage but wind, their bravery drunkenness. Fasting for them means dissolution; sobriety, panic. Nor has your master any force of ships on the sea. I alone have really stout sailors, and I will attack him with my fleets, destroy his maritime cities, and reduce to ashes those which have a river near them. Tell me, how with his small forces will he be able to resist me even on land? His son was there; his wife was there; his Saxons, Swabians, Bavarians, and Italians were all there with him; and yet they had not the skill nor the strength to take one little city that resisted them. How then will they resist me when I come followed by as many forces as there are 'Corn fields on Gargarus, grapes on Lesbian vine,/Waves in the ocean, stars in heaven that shine?' " [Ovid]

I wanted to answer and make such a speech in our defence as his boasting deserved; but he would not let me and added this final insult: "You are not Romans but Lombards." He even then was anxious to say more and waved his hand to secure my silence, but I was worked up and cried: "History tells us that Romulus, from whom the Romans get their name, was a fratricide born in adultery. He made a place of refuge for himself and received into it insolvent debtors, runaway slaves, murderers, and men who deserved death for their crimes. This was the sort of crowd whom he enrolled as citizens and gave them the name of Romans. From this nobility are descended those men whom you style 'rulers of the world.' But we Lombards, Saxons, Franks, Lotharingians, Bavarians, Swabians, and Burgundians, so despise these fellows that when we are angry with an enemy we can find nothing more insulting to say than 'You Roman!' For us in the word Roman is comprehended every form of lowness, timidity, avarice, luxury, falsehood, and vice. You say that we are unwarlike and know nothing of horsemanship. Well, if the sins of the Christians merit that you keep this stiff neck, the next war will prove what manner of men you are, and how warlike we."

Nicephorus, exasperated by these words, commanded the long narrow table to be removed and then calling for silence with his hand ordered me to return to my hateful abode, or, to speak more truly, to my prison. There two days later, as a result of my indignation as well as of heat and thirst, I fell seriously ill. Indeed there was not one of my companions who, having drunk from the same cup with me, did not fear that his last day was approaching. Why, I ask, should they not sicken? Their drink instead of good wine was brackish water; their bed was not hay, straw, or even earth, but hard marble; their pillow was a stone; their draughty house kept out neither heat nor rain nor cold. Salvation herself, to use a common expression, if she had poured all her favors on them, could not have saved them. Weakened therefore by my own tribulations and those of my companions I called in our warden, or rather my persecutor, and by prayers and bribes induced him to take the following letter to the emperor's brother:

"Bishop Liudprand to Leo, chancellor and marshal of the palace. If his serene highness the emperor intends to grant the request for which I came, then the sufferings I am now enduring shall not exhaust my patience: my master however must be informed by letter and messenger that my stay here is not useless. On the other hand, if a refusal is contemplated, there is a Venetian merchantman in harbor here just about to start. Let him permit me as a sick man to go on board, so that if the time of my dissolution be at hand, my native land may at least receive my corpse."

Leo read my letter and gave me an audience four days later. In accordance with their rule their wisest men, strong in Attic eloquence, sat with him to discuss your request, namely, Basil the chief chamberlain, the chief secretary, the chief master of the wardrobe, and two other dignitaries. They began their discourse as follows:

"Tell us, brother, the reason that induced you to take the trouble to come here."

When I told them that it was on account of the marriage which was to be the ground for a lasting peace, they said: "It is unheard of that a daughter born in the purple of an emperor born in the purple should contract a foreign marriage. Still, great as is your demand, you shall have what you want if you give what is proper—Ravenna, namely, and Rome with all the adjoining territories from thence to our possessions. If you desire friendship without the marriage, let your master permit Rome to be free, and hand over to their former lord the princes of Capua and Benevento, who were formerly slaves of our holy empire and are now rebels."

To this I answered: "Even you cannot but know that my master rules over Slavonian princes who are far more powerful than Peter king of the Bulgarians [927–969] who has married the daughter of the Emperor Christopher."[8]

"Ah," said they, "but Christopher was not born in the purple."

"As for Rome," I went on, "for whose freedom you are so noisily eager, who is her master? To whom does she pay tribute? Was she not formerly enslaved to harlots? And while you were sleeping, nay powerless, did not my master the august emperor free her from that foul servitude? Constantine [d. 337], the august emperor who founded this city and called it after his

[8] Christopher, eldest son of Romanus Lecapenus and co-emperor until his untimely death in 931 (*Camb. Med. Hist.*, IV, p. 143).

name, as being ruler of the world made many offerings to the Holy Roman Apostolic Church, not only in Italy, but in almost all the western kingdoms as well as those in the east and south, in Greece, Judaea, Persia, Mesopotamia, Babylonia, Egypt, Libya, as his own special regulations testify, preserved in our country. In Italy, in Saxony, in Bavaria, and in all my master's realms, everything that belongs to the Church of the Blessed Apostles has been handed over to those Holy Apostles' vicar. And if my master has kept back a single city, farm, vassal or slave, then I have denied God. Why does not your emperor do the same? Why does he not restore to the Apostolic Church what lies in his kingdoms and thereby himself increase the richness and freedom which it already owes to my master's exertions and generosity?"

"He will do so," said the chief chamberlain Basil, "when Rome and the Roman Church shall be so ordered as he wishes."

Then said I: "A certain man having suffered much injury from another, approached God with these words: 'Lord, avenge me upon my adversary.' To whom the Lord said: 'I will do so on the day when I shall render to each man according to his works.' 'How late that day will be!' the man replied."

At that everyone except the emperor's brother burst into laughter. Then they broke off the discussion and ordered me to be taken back to my detestable dwelling place and to be carefully guarded until the day of the Holy Apostles, a feast which all religious persons duly observe.

[Nicephorus was murdered in 969 by his wife Theophano and his nephew John Tzimisces.]


## 3    *Gerbert of Aurillac (Pope Sylvester II)*


*Gerbert was born about 940 in Aurillac, a village of the province of Auvergne, now the department of Cantal, in south central France. He received his early training at the monastery of St. Géraud in his home town and in 967 went to Spain for further education. Gerbert so impressed Pope John XIII when they met in Rome in 970 that*

*the pontiff sent the brilliant young scholar to the court of Otto I,
where he became tutor to the youthful Otto II. Gerbert left the
court in 972 and spent most of the decade in Reims, where he pursued his research interests: dialectic, astronomy, music, and mathe-
matics. He is credited with the introduction of the abacus to the
area of Western Europe outside Spain.*

*In 981 Otto II made Gerbert abbot of Bobbio in northwest Italy
because of his skill as an administrator, but Gerbert left there shortly
after the emperor's death in 983. Upon the accession of the three-
year-old Otto III, Gerbert was called upon by the king's mother
Theophano and grandmother Adelaide to keep the German ecclesiastical hierarchy loyal to the young monarch against the onslaught
of Henry the Wrangler of Bavaria (d. 995) who wanted to act as
co-king. Gerbert was so persuasive among the nobles and prelates to
whom he appealed that the Empress Theophano assumed the guardianship of her son, and Henry was excluded.*

*When Hugh Capet was elected king of France in 987, Gerbert
became his principal secretary and adviser. In 991 he was consecrated bishop of Reims, and after six years in that office he returned
to the German court. Otto III, crowned emperor in 996 at the age
of sixteen, became an eager pupil of Gerbert's in 997 and bestowed
upon his tutor the estate of Sasbach near Strasbourg. Letter II below
was despatched from this area. Letter I was issued by the emperor
as he was setting out for Italy in October, 997, and Gerbert joined
him there. Here the Archbishop of Reims was made Archbishop of
Ravenna, and in 999 upon the death of Pope Gregory V, he succeeded to the Papacy, taking the name Sylvester II. The choice was
significant, for Sylvester I (314-335) was pope when the Emperor
Constantine supposedly gave to the western Church dominion over
Rome, Italy, and the provinces. The so-called "Donation of Constantine"* (Constitutum Constantini), *though a forgery of the eighth century, was generally accepted as part of canon law until 1440 when
Lorenzo Valla (1406-1457) questioned its authenticity, and it was not
definitively classed as a fraud until the 18th century. Only during
the Ottonian period was the validity of the Donation attacked (see
D.O. III. 389, p. 63 below).*

*By taking the name Sylvester II, Gerbert was in effect announcing
his close ties with Otto III and his hope for a renovated Roman
Empire. During his short reign (999-1003) he was a vigorous ad-*

*ministrator, who sought to strengthen the Papacy by aligning it on the side of the Emperor. Gerbert was one of the most remarkable men of the tenth century—equally effective as teacher, scholar, and administrator.*

---

I. *Emperor Otto III writes a letter for himself inviting Gerbert to become his teacher and enclosing an original verse* (Aachen, October 21, 997).

Emperor Otto to Gerbert, His Teacher

Otto himself writes Gerbert, most skilled of masters and crowned in the three branches of philosophy.[1]

We wish to attach to our person the excellence of your very loving self, so revered by all, and we seek to affiliate with ourself the perennial steadfastness of such a patron because the extent of your philosophical knowledge has always been for Our Simplicity an authority not to be scorned. Not to be ambiguous but to enjoy plain speaking with you, we have firmly resolved and arranged that this letter shall make clear to you our desire as to the extent of our choice and the singleness of our request in order that your expert knowledge may be zealous in correcting us, though not more than usual, unlearned and badly educated as we are, both in writing and speaking, and that with respect to the commonwealth you may offer advice of the highest trustworthiness.

We desire you to show your aversion to Saxon ignorance by not refusing this suggestion of our wishes, but even more we desire you to stimulate Our Greek Subtlety to zeal for study, because if there is anyone who will arouse it, he will find some shred of the diligence of the Greeks in it. Thanks to this, we

[1] Natural (physics), moral (ethics), and rational (logic). This was the Platonic division of philosophy known through Isidore's *Etymologiae* II.xxiv.3–8. Gerbert, however, followed the Aristotelian division known through Boethius, Cassiodorus, and a later section (pars. 9–16) of the same chapter of *Etymologiae* [Lattin's note].

SOURCE. Gerbert of Aurillac, *The Letters of Gerbert, with His Papal Privileges as Sylvester II*, translated by Harriet Pratt Lattin, (New York: Columbia University Press, 1961) pp. 294–297. Reprinted by permission of publisher and author.

humbly ask that the flame of your knowledge may sufficiently fan our spirit until, with God's aid, you cause the lively genius of the Greeks to shine forth.

Pray explain to us the book on arithmetic[2] so that when fully taught by its lessons we may learn something of the attainments of the ancients.

Whether it pleases you to act upon this invitation, or displeases you, may Your Paternity not postpone making a reply to us by letter.

Farewell.

> Verses have I never made
> Nor in such study ever stayed
> When to its practice myself I apply
> And can write successfully,
> As many men as has Lorraine,
> To you, then, songs I'll send the same.

II.   *Gerbert accepts Otto III's invitation to join his court as a teacher* (near Sasbach, October 25, 997).[3]

Gerbert to Otto Caesar

Gerbert, archbishop of Rheims,[4] by the grace of God, [sends] whatever is worthy so great an emperor to the ever august glorious Lord Otto.

Not because of our merits, though perchance because of solemn vows, are we able to make answer to your surpassing kindness that deems us worthy of perpetual obedience to you. If we are aglow with the slightest spark of knowledge, it re-

---

[2] Probably a manuscript of Boethius *De arithmetica*, sent as a gift by Gerbert to Otto . . . written on purple parchment in gold and silver letters, a truly royal book. The manuscript, a product of the school of Tours, had been written for Charles the Bald [840–877] soon after 832 but before his coronation as emperor [Lattin's note].

[3] This Letter . . . was undoubtedly written immediately after the receipt of Letter [I], which it answers. The latest date when Otto III is known to have been at Aachen was October 27, 997 (DO III 262) [Lattin's note].

[4] Gerbert here reminds Otto III to address him not merely as teacher (*magister*) but by a title corresponding to the dignity of archbishop of Rheims [Lattin's note].

dounds to your glory through the excellence of your father who matched it.

What shall I say? We are not bringing our own treasures to yours, but rather are giving back what we once received, some of which you have enjoyed already,[5] some of which you are very soon to enjoy as is evidenced by the honest and useful invitation, so worthy of Your Majesty. For, unless you were not firmly convinced that the power of numbers contained both the origins of all things in itself and explained all from itself,[6] you would not be hastening to a full and perfect knowledge of them with such zeal. Furthermore, unless you were embracing the seriousness of moral philosophy, humility, the guardian of all virtues, would not thus be impressed upon your words.

Not silent, moreover, is the subtlety of a mind conscious of itself since, as I might say, oratorically you have shown its oratorical capabilities as flowing from itself and its Greek fountain. I do not know what more evidence of the divine there can be than that a man, Greek by birth, Roman by empire, as if by hereditary right seeks to recapture for himself the treasures of Greek and Roman wisdom.

Therefore, Caesar, we obey the imperial edicts not only in this, but also in all things whatsoever Your Divine Majesty has decreed. For we who consider nothing sweeter among human affairs than your command cannot fail in obedience to you.

[5] A reference to their learned discussions earlier in 997 [Lattin's note].

[6] The verses on the Boethius manuscript sent to Otto III by Gerbert [see preceding letter] contain the same idea. St. Augustine in various *Sermons* (lii, cclii, cclxiv; cclxx, PL XXXVIII, 352, 353, 1177–78, 1216, 1240) discusses the power of number, likewise Martianus Capella VII.731ff., Boethius *De arithmetica* I.ii, and Macrobius *Commentarii in somnium Scipionis,* who writes (I.vi.8), "This number one, the beginning and end of all things, though it itself knows no beginning or end, pertains to the highest god and separates our knowledge of him from knowledge of the things and powers following" [Lattin's note].

# 4                    *Hroswitha of Gandersheim*

*Hroswitha (also spelt Hrosvitha, Roswitha, and Hrotsuit) was both a dramatist and historian. She was probably born around the year 935 and died between 1001 and 1002. Some time before 959 she entered Gandersheim, a Benedictine convent founded in 881. Such convents were often filled with the daughters of important families and were frequently centers of education and learning. Hroswitha amply demonstrates her familiarity with classical authors and quotes from them freely. Her works include five plays besides* Callimachus, *eight narrative religious poems, and two historical works—*Carmen de gestis Oddonis (The Deeds of Otto) *and* De primordiis et fundatoribus coenobii Gandersheimensis. *The first of these historical works is a poem which begins with the reign of Henry I in 919 and concludes with a fragment dealing with the years between 962 and 967. The second deals with the history of Gandersheim from its foundation to the year 919.*

---

## CALLIMACHUS

### *Argument*

### *The Resurrection of Drusiana and Callimachus*

Callimachus cherishes a guilty passion for Drusiana, not only while she is alive but after she has died in the Lord. He dies from the bite of a serpent, but, thanks to the prayers of Saint John the Apostle, he is restored to life, together with Drusiana, and is born again in Christ.

SOURCE. Roswitha of Gandersheim, "Callimachus," *The Plays of Roswitha*, trans. Christopher St. John, pseud. of Christabel Marshall (London: Chatto & Windus, Ltd., 1923), pp. 49–63. Reprinted by permission of the publisher.

*Characters*

CALLIMACHUS
FRIENDS TO CALLIMACHUS
DRUSIANA
ANDRONICUS
FORTUNATUS
THE APOSTLE JOHN


## CALLIMACHUS


### Scene I

CALLIMACHUS. My friends, a word with you.

FRIENDS. We are at your service as long as you please.

CALLIMACHUS. I should prefer to speak with you apart from the crowd.

FRIENDS. What pleases you, pleases us.

CALLIMACHUS. Then we will go to some quieter place where no one will interrupt us.

FRIENDS. Just as you like.


### Scene II

CALLIMACHUS. For a long time now I have been in great trouble. I hope that by confiding in you I shall find relief.

FRIENDS. When a man tells his friends of his sufferings it is only fair that they should try to share them.

CALLIMACHUS. I would to heaven that you could lighten this load upon my heart!

FRIENDS. Well, tell us precisely what is wrong. We will grieve with you, if we must. If not, we can do our best to distract your mind.

CALLIMACHUS. I love—

FRIENDS. What do you love?

CALLIMACHUS. A thing of beauty, a thing of grace!

FRIENDS. That is too vague! How can we tell from this what is the object of your love?

CALLIMACHUS. Woman.

FRIENDS. Ah, now you say "woman" we all understand!

CALLIMACHUS. By woman, I mean a woman.

FRIENDS. Clearer still! But it is impossible to give an opinion on a subject until the subject is defined. So name the woman.

CALLIMACHUS. Drusiana.

FRIENDS. What? The wife of Prince Andronicus?

CALLIMACHUS. Yes.

FRIENDS. Nothing can come of that. She has been baptized.

CALLIMACHUS. What do I care, if I can win her love.

FRIENDS. You cannot.

CALLIMACHUS. What makes you say so?

FRIENDS. You are crying for the moon.

CALLIMACHUS. Am I the first to do so? Have I not the example of many others to encourage me?

FRIENDS. Now listen. This woman you sigh for is a follower of the holy Apostle John, and has devoted herself entirely to God. They say she will not even go to the bed of Andronicus although he is a devout Christian. Is it likely that she will listen to you?

CALLIMACHUS. I came to you for consolation, and instead you drive me to despair!

FRIENDS. We should be poor friends if we consoled and flattered you at the expense of the truth.

CALLIMACHUS. Since you refuse to advise me, I will go to her and pour out my soul in words that would melt a heart of stone!

FRIENDS. Fool! It is hopeless!

CALLIMACHUS. I defy the stars!

FRIENDS. We shall see.

## Scene III

CALLIMACHUS. Drusiana, listen to me! Drusiana, my deepest heart's love!

DRUSIANA. Your words amaze me, Callimachus. What can you want of me?

CALLIMACHUS. You are amazed?

DRUSIANA. I am astounded.

CALLIMACHUS. First I want to speak of love!

DRUSIANA. Love! What love?

CALLIMACHUS. That love with which I love you above all created things.

DRUSIANA. Why should you love me? You are not of my kin. There is no legal bond between us.

CALLIMACHUS. It is your beauty.

DRUSIANA. My beauty?

CALLIMACHUS. Yes.

DRUSIANA. What is my beauty to you?

CALLIMACHUS. But little now—it is that which tortures me— but I hope that it may be much before long.

DRUSIANA. Not a word more. Leave me at once, for it is a sin to listen to you now that I understand your devilish meaning.

CALLIMACHUS. My Drusiana, do not kill me with your looks. Do not drive away one who worships you, but give back love for love.

DRUSIANA. Wicked, insidious words! They fall on deaf ears. Your love disgusts me. Understand I despise you!

CALLIMACHUS. You cannot make me angry, because I know that you would own my passion moves you if you were not ashamed.

DRUSIANA. It moves me to indignation, nothing else.

CALLIMACHUS. That feeling will not last.

DRUSIANA. I shall not change, be sure of that.

CALLIMACHUS. I would not be too sure.

DRUSIANA. You frantic, foolish man! Do not deceive yourself! Why delude yourself with vain hopes? What madness leads you to think that I shall yield? I have renounced even what is lawful —my husband's bed!

CALLIMACHUS. I call heaven and earth to witness that if you do not yield I will never rest from the fight for you. I will be as cunning as the serpent. I will use all my skill and strength to trap you.

## Scene IV

DRUSIANA. O Lord Jesus, what use is my vow of chastity? My beauty has all the same made this man love me. Pity my fears, O Lord. Pity the grief which has seized me. I know not what to do. If I tell anyone what has happened, there will be disorder in the city on my account; if I keep silence, only Thy grace can protect me from falling into the net spread for me. O Christ, take me to Thyself. Let me die swiftly. Save me from being the ruin of a soul!

ANDRONICUS. Drusiana, Drusiana! Christ, what blow has fallen on me! Drusiana is dead. Run one of you and fetch the holy man John.

## Scene V

JOHN. Why do you weep, my son?

ANDRONICUS. Oh, horrible! O Lord, that life should suddenly become so hateful!

JOHN. What troubles you?

ANDRONICUS. Drusiana, your disciple, Drusiana—

JOHN. She has passed from the sight of men?

ANDRONICUS. Yes. I am desolate.

JOHN. It is not right to mourn so bitterly for those whose souls we know rejoice in peace.

ANDRONICUS. God knows I do not doubt that her soul is in eternal joy, and that her incorrupt body will rise again. What grieves me so sorely is that in my presence just now she prayed for death. She begged she might die.

JOHN. You know her reason?

ANDRONICUS. I know it, and will tell you when I am less sick with grief.

JOHN. Come. We must celebrate the funeral rites with proper ceremony.

ANDRONICUS. There is a marble tomb near here in which the

body shall be laid, and our steward Fortunatus shall guard her grave.

JOHN. It is right that she should be interred with honour. God rest her soul in peace.

## Scene VI

CALLIMACHUS. Fortunatus, Fortunatus, what is to become of me? Death itself cannot quench my love for Drusiana!

FORTUNATUS. Poor wretch!

CALLIMACHUS. I shall die if you do not help me.

FORTUNATUS. How can I help you?

CALLIMACHUS. In this. You can let me look on her, dead.

FORTUNATUS. Up to now the body is sound and whole, I reckon because it was not wasted with disease. As you know she was taken in a moment by a fever.

CALLIMACHUS. Oh, how happy I should be if I might see for myself.

FORTUNATUS. If you are willing to pay me well, you can do what you like.

CALLIMACHUS. Here, take all I have with me, and be sure that I will give you more, much more, later.

FORTUNATUS. Quick, then! We'll go to the tomb.

CALLIMACHUS. You cannot go quickly enough for me.

## Scene VII

FORTUNATUS. There lies the body. The face is not like the face of a corpse. The limbs show no sign of decay. You can take her to your heart.[1]

---

[1] *Abutere ut libet* of the original does not mean "You can take her to your heart." Rather it means "misuse (abuse or make use of) her as you will." Hroswitha therefore seems to have been more realistic and less romantic than her translator. Callimachus has been compared with Shakespeare's Romeo (see Charles Magnin, *Théâtre de Hrosvitha* [Paris: Duprat, 1845], xlv-xlvii) because both men enter the tomb of their dead sweetheart, but the intention of Callimachus is clearly that of a rapist, whereas Romeo—the grieving husband—only seeks a last kiss.

CALLIMACHUS. O Drusiana, Drusiana, I worshipped you with my whole soul! I yearned from my very bowels to embrace you! And you repulsed me, and thwarted my desire. Now you are in my power, now I can wound you with my kisses, and pour out my love on you.[2]

FORTUNATUS. Take care! A monstrous serpent! It is coming towards us!

CALLIMACHUS. A curse on me! And on you, Fortunatus, who led me on and urged me to this infamy. Wretch may you die from the serpent's bite! Terror and remorse are killing me.

## Scene VIII

JOHN. Come, Andronicus, let us go to Drusiana's tomb, and commend her soul to Christ in prayer.

ANDRONICUS. It is like your holiness not to forget one who trusted in you.

JOHN. Behold! The invisible God appears to us, made visible in the form of a beautiful youth.

ANDRONICUS (To the Spectators). Tremble.[3]

JOHN. Lord Jesus, why hast Thou deigned to manifest Thyself to Thy servants in this place?

GOD. To raise Drusiana from the dead, and with her him who lies outside her tomb, have I come, that in them My Name may be glorified.

ANDRONICUS. How swiftly He was caught up again into heaven!

JOHN. I cannot altogether understand what this means.

ANDRONICUS. Let us go on to the tomb. It may be that there what is now obscure will become clear.

---

[2] Again the translator softens the original: Nunc in mea situm est potestate quantislibet injuriis te velim lacessere—"Now it is within my power to arouse you with as many wounds as I wish." Nothing is said of love and kisses.

[3] This admonition to "spectators" in the manuscript seems inexplicable if Hroswitha wrote her plays to be read, not performed [St. John's note].

## Scene IX

JOHN. In Christ's name, what miracle is this? The sepulchre is open, and Drusiana's body has been cast forth. And near it lie two other corpses enlaced in a serpent's coils.

ANDRONICUS. I begin to understand. This is Callimachus, who while he lived was consumed with an unholy passion for Drusiana. It troubled her greatly and her distress brought on a fever. She prayed that she might die.

JOHN. Such was her love of chastity.

ANDRONICUS. After her death the wretched man, crazed with love, and stung by the defeat of his wicked plan, was still more inflamed by desire.

JOHN. Pitiable creature!

ANDRONICUS. I have no doubt that he bribed this unworthy servant to give him the opportunity for committing a detestable crime.

JOHN. It is not to be believed!

ANDRONICUS. But death struck both of them down before the deed was accomplished.[4]

JOHN. They met their deserts.

ANDRONICUS. What astonishes me most is that the Divine Voice should have promised the resurrection of him who planned the crime, and not of him who was only an accomplice. Maybe it is because the one, blinded by the passion of the flesh, knew not what he did, while the other sinned of deliberate malice.

JOHN. With what wonderful exactness the Supreme Judge examines the deeds of men! How even the scales in which He weighs the merits of each individual man! None can understand, none explain. Human wisdom cannot grasp the subtlety of the divine judgment.

ANDRONICUS. So we should be content to marvel at it, as it is not in our power to attain a precise knowledge of the causes of things.

---

[4] "Deed" does not render the Latin *scelus*, which means an outrageous act, an abominable crime.

JOHN. Often the sequel teaches us to understand better.

ANDRONICUS. Then, blessed John, do now what you were told to do. Raise Callimachus to life, and the knot of our perplexity may be untied.

JOHN. First I must invoke the name of Christ to drive away the serpent. Then Callimachus shall be raised.

ANDRONICUS. You are right; else the venom of the creature might do him fresh injury.

JOHN. Hence, savage monster! Away from this man, for now he is to serve Christ.

ANDRONICUS. Although the beast has no reason, it heeds your command.

JOHN. Not through my power, but through Christ's, it obeys me.

ANDRONICUS. Look! As swift as thought it has vanished!

JOHN. O God, the world cannot contain nor the mind of man comprehend the wonders of Thy incalculable unity, Thou Who alone art what Thou art! O Thou Who by mingling different elements canst create man, and by separating those elements again canst dissolve him, grant that the spirit and the body of this Callimachus may be joined once more, and that he may rise again wholly as he was, so that all looking on him may praise Thee, Who alone canst work miracles!

ANDRONICUS. Look! The breath of life stirs in him again, but he does not move.

JOHN. Callimachus! In the name of Christ, arise, and confess your sin! Do not keep back the smallest grain of truth. . . . What mad folly possessed you? That you should dare think of such a shameful outrage to the chaste dead!

CALLIMACHUS. Yes, I was mad; but this knave Fortunatus led me on.

JOHN. And now, most miserable man, confess! Were you so vile as to do what you desired?

CALLIMACHUS. No! I could think of it, but I could not do it.

JOHN. What prevented you?

CALLIMACHUS. I had hardly touched the lifeless body—I had hardly drawn aside the shroud, when that fellow there, who has been the spark to my fire, died from the serpent's poison.

ANDRONICUS. A good riddance!

CALLIMACHUS. At the same moment there appeared to me a young man, beautiful yet terrible, who reverently covered the corpse again. From his flaming face and breast burning coals flew out, and one of them, falling on me, touched my face. I heard a voice say, "Callimachus, die to live!" It was then I breathed my last.

JOHN. Oh, heavenly grace! God delights not in the damnation of the wicked.

CALLIMACHUS. You have heard the dreadful tale of my temptation. I beg you not to delay the merciful remedy.

JOHN. I will not delay it.

CALLIMACHUS. I am overwhelmed by the thought of my abominable crime. I repent with my whole heart, and bewail my sin.

JOHN. That is but right, for a great fault must be atoned for by a great repentance.

CALLIMACHUS. Oh, if I could lay bare my heart and show you the bitter anguish I suffer, you would pity me!

JOHN. Not so. Rather does your suffering fill me with joy, for I know that it will be your salvation.

CALLIMACHUS. I loathe the delights of the flesh, and all the sins of my past life.

JOHN. That is well.

CALLIMACHUS. I truly repent my foul deed.

JOHN. Again that is well.

CALLIMACHUS. I am filled with such remorse that I have no desire to live unless I can be born again in Christ and changed.

JOHN. I do not doubt that heavenly grace is at work in you.

CALLIMACHUS. Oh, hasten then to help a man in dire need! Give me some comfort! Help me to throw off the grief which crushes me! Show me how a Pagan may change into a Christian, a fornicator into a chaste man! Oh, set my feet on the way of truth! Teach me to live mindful of the divine promises!

JOHN. Now blessed be the only Son of God, Who made Himself partaker of our frailty, and showed you mercy, my son Callimachus, by striking you down with the death which has brought you to the true life. So has He saved the creature He made in His own image from the death of the soul.

ANDRONICUS. Most strange, most wonderful miracle!

JOHN. O Christ, redemption of the world, and sinners' atonement, I have no words to praise Thee! The sweetness of Thy compassion amazes me. Now Thou dost win the sinner with gentleness, now Thou dost chastise him with just severity, and callest on him to do penance.

ANDRONICUS. Glory to His divine goodness!

JOHN. Who would have presumed to hope that a man like this, intent on a wicked deed when death overtook him, would be raised to life again, and given the chance of making reparation! Blessed be Thy name for ever and ever, O Thou Who alone canst do these wondrous things!

ANDRONICUS. Holy John, give me some comfort too. The love I bear my dead wife will not let me rest until I have seen her also called back from the dead.

JOHN. Drusiana, our Lord Jesus Christ calls you back to life!

DRUSIANA. Glory and praise to Thee, O Lord, Who has made me live again!

CALLIMACHUS. Thanks be to that merciful power, my Drusiana, through which you, who left this life in such sorrow, rise again in joy!

DRUSIANA. Venerable father John, you have restored to life Callimachus, who loved me sinfully. Should you not also raise from the dead the man who betrayed my buried body?

CALLIMACHUS. Apostle of Christ, do not believe it! Will you release from the fetters of death this evil creature, this traitor, who led me away and persuaded me to venture on that horrible deed?

JOHN. You should not wish to deprive him of divine mercy, my son.

CALLIMACHUS. He tried to ruin me! He is not worthy of resurrection!

JOHN. We are taught by our faith that man must forgive his fellow-man if he would be forgiven by God.

ANDRONICUS. That is true.

JOHN. Remember that when the only Son of God, the Virgin's first-born, the one man born without a stain, came into this world, He found us all bowed under the heavy weight of sin.

ANDRONICUS. True again.

JOHN. And though not one of us was guiltless, He deprived no one of His mercy, but offered Himself for all, and for all laid down His life in love.

ANDRONICUS. Had the Innocent One not been slain, none of us would have been saved.

JOHN. He cannot rejoice in the damnation of those whom He bought with His blood.

ANDRONICUS. To Him be praise!

JOHN. This is why we must not grudge the grace of God to anyone. It is no merit of ours if it abounds in ourselves.

CALLIMACHUS. Your rebuke makes me ashamed.

JOHN. Yet it is not for me to oppose you. Drusiana, inspired by God Himself shall raise this man.

DRUSIANA. Divine Essence without material form, Who has made man in Thine own image and breathed into this clay the spirit of life, bring back the vital heat to the body of Fortunatus, that our triple resurrection may glorify the adorable Trinity.

JOHN. Amen.

DRUSIANA. Fortunatus, awake, and in the name of Christ burst the bonds of death.

FORTUNATUS. Who wakes me? Who takes my hand? Who calls me back to life?

JOHN. Drusiana.

FORTUNATUS. How can that be? Only a few days since she died.

JOHN. Yes, but now, through the power of Christ, she lives again.

FORTUNATUS. And is that Callimachus who stands there? By his sober and pious look one would think he is no longer dying of love for his Drusiana!

JOHN. All that is changed. Now he loves and serves Christ.

FORTUNATUS. No!

JOHN. It is true.

FORTUNATUS. If it is as you say, if Drusiana has restored me to life and Callimachus believes in Christ, I reject life and choose death. I would rather not exist than see them swelling with grace and virtue!

JOHN. Oh, incredible envy of the devil! Oh, malice of the old serpent, who since he made our first parents taste death has never ceased to writhe at the glory of the righteous! Oh, Fortunatus, brimful of Satan's bitter gall, how much do you resemble the rotten tree that, bearing only bad fruit, must be cut down and cast into the fire! To the fire you must go, where, deprived of the society of those who fear God, you will be tormented without respite for ever.

ANDRONICUS. Look! Oh, look! His wounds have opened again. He has been taken at his word. He is dying.

JOHN. Let him die and go down to hell, who through envious spite rejected the gift of life.

ANDRONICUS. A terrible fate.

JOHN. Nothing is more terrible than envy, nothing more evil than pride.

ANDRONICUS. Both are vile.

JOHN. The man who is the victim of one is the victim of the other, for they have no separate existence.

ANDRONICUS. Please explain.

JOHN. The proud are envious, and the envious are proud. A jealous man cannot endure to hear others praised, and seeks to belittle those who are more perfect. He disdains to take a lower place, and arrogantly seeks to be put above his equals.

ANDRONICUS. That is clear.

JOHN. This wretched man's pride was wounded. He could not endure the humiliation of recognizing his inferiority to these two in whom he could not deny God had made more grace to shine.

ANDRONICUS. I understand now why his resurrection was not spoken of. It was known he would die again.

JOHN. He deserved to die twice, for to his crime of profaning the sacred grave entrusted to him, he added hatred and envy of those who had been restored to life.

ANDRONICUS. The wretched creature is dead now.

JOHN. Come, let us go—Satan must have his own. This day shall be kept as a festival in thanksgiving for the wonderful conversion of Callimachus. Men shall long speak of it, and of his resurrection from the dead, and of Drusiana, on whom his love brought misery. Let us give thanks to God, that just and penetrating Judge Who alone can search the heart and reins and reward or punish fairly.[5] To Him alone be honour, strength, glory, praise, and blessing, world without end. Amen.

[5] "Reins" mean kidneys.


5                              *Bernward of Hildesheim*


*Bernward was born about 960, but we do not know where. Nor do we know the identity of his parents except that they may have belonged to the Saxon nobility. In 993, Bernward was consecrated Bishop of Hildesheim by Archbishop Willigis of Mainz. Willigis and Bernward fell into a dispute over the boundary line of their respective dioceses, and it was for that reason that Bernward went to Rome in November, 1000. The trip was a success, for Pope Sylvester II upheld Bernward's claims against Willigis. Bernward also received the benefit of seeing the monuments of ancient Rome at first hand, which had a profound effect on his own artistic plans for the beautification of Hildesheim. Some of the art works of Hildesheim can be seen in Plates 4 to 10.*


## IN THE SERVICE OF OTTO III

On the second of November, 1000, the priests and people of Hildesheim assembled to bid farewell to their bishop. With Thangmar he went over the Alps by way of Trent, because that appeared to be the easier route.[1] He reached the Eternal City two months later, on the fourth of January, 1001.

[1] Thangmar, about ten years older than Bernward, was *primicerius* at Hildesheim, that is, provost of the cathedral chapter, when Bernward was in school there. Subsequently he became episcopal secretary (*notarius*) and archivist (*bibliothecarius*). Thangmar wrote a biography of Bernward which is our principal source for his life. Thietmar, Bishop of Merseburg 1009–1018, is another important source for Bernward's times. His chronicle tells us more about eastern Germany than any other writer of the period. SOURCE. Francis J. Tschan, *Saint Bernward of Hildesheim*. (Notre Dame, Indiana: The University of Notre Dame, 1942–1952), I, 106–113. Reprinted by permission of the publisher.

PLATE IV. Exterior of St. Michael's Church at Hildes—
heim (Marburg—Art Reference Bureau).

PLATE V. Interior of St. Michael's Church at Hildesheim, the nave looking west (Marburg Art Reference Bureau).

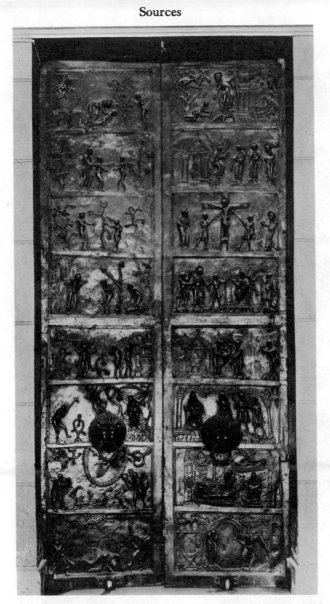

PLATE VI. Bronze doors of Cathedral Church at Hildesheim (Marburg —Art Reference Bureau).

PLATE VII. Expulsion scene from bronze doors, Cathedral Church at Hildesheim (Marburg–Art Reference Bureau).

PLATE VIII.  Bronze column from Cathedral Church at Hildesheim
(Marburg—Art Reference Bureau).

PLATE IX.  River god on bronze column at Cathedral Church at Hildesheim (Marburg—Art Reference Bureau).

PLATE X.   Relief from bronze column of Cathedral Church at Hildesheim
(Marburg—Art Reference Bureau).

On hearing of Bernward's coming, Otto left his palace on the Aventine to meet him at Saint Peter's, a distance of about two Roman miles. After affectionate greetings the bishop went to the lodgings which the emperor had provided in advance for his comfort. The next morning Bernward was to enjoy further evidence of the esteem in which he was held—when he reached Otto's palace both the pope [Sylvester II] and emperor were there to greet him. The conversation, beginning with a general discussion of the state of affairs of Germany, continued to the Gandersheim controversy, and before they parted Otto arranged for an early hearing of Bernward's cause against Willigis.[2] The emperor also insisted that the bishop occupy quarters near his palace on the Aventine.

The Saxon Bernward must have marvelled at the eastern splendors of Otto's palace. High on the Aventine, once the seat of the plebeians, it overlooked the city of the Caesars, whose glories its lord wished to revive. The emperor, as the son of the Grecian princess Theophano, chose to wear Byzantine costume, decorated with detailed patterns mingling picturings from the Apocalypse with figures from the animal world. He received his guests with punctilious solemnity, and they addressed him as "emperor of all emperors" and, according to ancient Roman fashion, by the names of his subject peoples, *Saxonicus, Romanus, Italicus*.[3] His officers were numerous and all possessed titles echoing the classical past or Byzantine present. Consuls and senators, *magistri et comites imperialis militiae* [commanders and commandants of the imperial army] and even a *praefectus navalis* [naval commander], although Otto had no fleet, mingled with *protospatharii* [court dignitaries] and the two clerical *logothetoi* [imperial chancellors]—the chancellor, Heribert of Cologne, and Bishop Leo of Vercelli. To show the universality of his realm Otto was

---

[2] Gandersheim was on the boundary line between the lands of the Archbishop of Mainz (Willigis) and those of Hildesheim. This was the subject of a long drawn-out dispute, which was finally settled in 1007 by Henry II in favor of Hildesheim.

[3] Cf. Gerbert's concept of the Roman Empire in Carl Erdmann, "The Ottonian Empire as *Imperium Romanum*," p. 97, and see also. Plate 12 showing the emperor receiving homage from the four parts of the empire—Germania, Alemannia, Francia, and Italia.

also served by officials whose titles came from Frankish sources. In the city a patrician once more ruled with a prefect who, though responsible to the emperor, was the papal *Vogt* [advocate]. As in Ottonian Germany so in Rome and Italy the state and Church were closely linked together, for Gerbert needed Otto's protection, such as it was, and Otto constantly needed Gerbert's shrewd, if not wise counsel.

Bernward's time was occupied that January by the synod which apparently was not hesitant about deciding in his favor, and by Otto's controversy with the burghers of Tivoli. No less successful was Bernward's intervention in the emperor's difficulties. One of the several rebellions which greeted the emperor when he returned from Germany in November, less than two months before Bernward's arrival, was that of Tivoli. The men of that city, secure in the natural defenses of their town in the Sabine Hills, had ventured to dispute Otto's authority, and had been closely besieged, but would not yield. Otto was promptly called to take personal charge of the operations. He came with the pope, Saint Romuald who was one of the ascetics in whom he had great faith, and Bernward.[4] After surveying the situation and receiving much advice from those who had been carrying on the siege, Otto took Bernward aside to consult with him. Thangmar has preserved the bishop's formal advice. He was grieved to think that Otto, whom he loved more dearly than his own life, should be so distressed and, although he himself yearned to return to his homeland, he was resolved not to leave Otto's side until Tivoli and its citizens had submitted to imperial authority. He told Otto to press the siege with greater vigor, a course which he evidently hoped would facilitate negotiations.

The emperor adopted his tutor's advice, and the siege lines were tightly drawn. No one could go in or out of the city. A few days later when Bernward, the pope and Saint Romuald went up to its portals, the burghers received them with respect. A truce was negotiated and the following day the two prelates led the leading citizens of Tivoli to Otto's palace. Naked except for loin cloths, carrying their swords in their right hands and

---

[4] St. Romuald (951–1027) was an ascetic monk at the monastery of Camaldoli, between Florence and Rimini.

besoms in their left,[5] the burghers came into the imperial presence to submit and not to negotiate. They would not even ask that their lives be spared. The emperor might use the sword on those he found guilty or, if he was merciful, might have them publicly whipped. He might command that their city be levelled with the ground, but so long as they lived they would never again oppose the emperor's commands. Such abject submission after weeks of stubborn resistance must have been a matter of previous agreement with the ecclesiastical diplomats. Both the pope and Bernward participated in the council which Otto immediately convened to decide what course to take with the rebels. The city was spared, and its people were returned into favor with the warning never again to oppose his imperial majesty.

Peace was no sooner established with the men of Tivoli than those of Rome rebelled. Long fearful that the smaller towns about them would rise to dispute their dominance, the Romans were angered at the terms the Tivolitans had won. Two instigators, one of whom had formerly enjoyed the emperor's favor, induced the Romans to revolt in February. They shut the gates of the city, forbade all trade, murdered some of Otto's friends and besieged the emperor in his palace on the Aventine. Proceedings of such a kind had to be met with stern measures if the imperial prestige, so lately reestablished, was to be maintained, and Bernward rose to the occasion. He proceeded to inspire and prepare the men of Otto's palace for the fight. He preached encouragingly to them, heard their confessions and gave them communion. Then he blessed the palatines [palace guards] with the Holy Lance given to Henry the Fowler by Rudolf of Burgundy, a standard which for years had inspired the German army.[6] Imbedded in it were nails with which Christ had been fastened to His cross. Bernward carried the Lance on the following day when he and Otto led out the soldiers to break the Roman investment.

Terrifying, says Thangmar, was the army which confronted the Romans. Bernward prayed fervently to himself that peace should come without bloodshed, and on the next day the rebels

[5] A besom is a broom made out of a bundle of twigs.
[6] See note 3, p. 17.

sued for peace, largely through the intervention of the dukes of Tuscany and Bavaria, who were encamped near Rome. When they came to Otto to renew their oaths of fidelity, the emperor addressed them from a tower of his castle. The speech was characteristic of his grandiose plans to restore the ancient glories of the Augustan empire, and yet revealed also the disillusionment which had come upon the young emperor:

"Hearken to your father's words and keep them carefully in your hearts. Are you not my Romans? For you indeed I left my fatherland and also forsook my kin. For love of you I rejected my Saxons and all the Germans, my blood. I led you into remote parts of my empire in which your fathers, when they ruled the world, never set foot, that I might spread your name and glory to the ends of the earth. I adopted you as my sons. I preferred you to all. For your sake, because I put you before all, I brought on myself the envy and hatred of all. And now, for all this, you have rejected your father. You have cruelly put my friends to death. You have excluded me even though you could not shut me out because I embrace you with a father's love and will never suffer you to be banished from my affection. I know, indeed, who are the instigators of this sedition and I fix my eyes upon them. Although the eyes of all are publicly upon them, they are not abashed. Perish the thought that those most true to me, in whose innocence I glory, should be contaminated by association with these wretches and not be distinguished from them."

The Romans were moved to tears and, swearing they would make satisfaction, they dragged the two instigators, naked and half dead, to Otto's feet. Thangmar makes no comment on Bernward's reaction. Bernward was far too discreet a man to be moved to anything but silent pity for the young emperor, visibly broken in health as well as in spirit.[7] He contented himself with admonitions such as a prelate and respected tutor could venture to offer one in exalted position. Gerbert, the pope, might have

[7] Otto III died of smallpox on January 24, 1002, at the age of twenty-two. His body was brought back to Aachen, where he was entombed in the choir of St. Mary's church.

presumed to be plain of speech, but he chose to nourish the imagination of the Graeco-Saxon emperor.

Bernward, however, derived from this Italian sojourn much more than the satisfaction of having been sustained in his controversy with Willigis. Artistically this visit accomplished the same purpose for him as the imperial connection, established in 962 between the north and the south, had for his countrymen. Formerly their impressions of the antique came for the most part indirectly from Roman remains, through the Church and through . . . Carolingian [remains]. Now, like many another German ecclesiastic and noble before and after him, Bernward with his own eyes could look directly upon the glories of . . . ancient . . . Rome [and therefore] his sense of the antique could be refined as it never would have been if he had lived and traveled only in Germany. Although many of the buildings of the classical city lay in ruins or had been remodelled to serve other purposes, this antique [site] had lost none of its values. It lived, not fixed in museums or galleries, but in the everyday experience of people. And for a man of religious sense in the millennial year its effects were all the more telling because it had been permeated by [Christianity].[8] Memorials of the martyrs were everywhere about him. Churches and shrines of venerable antiquity and associations were open ready to receive him.[9] Art treasures of fabulous worth were his to look upon at almost every step.

Bernward, however, was not a tourist ready to stroll about with guidebook in hand.[10] He had come to Rome with weighty matters on his mind to see the two most important personages in the world of his day, and was not entirely free to go about

[8] The year 1000 did not cause widespread consternation as was previously assumed. Predictions of the Second Coming and the Last Judgment were made well before and well after the turn of the millennium.

[9] About the year 1000 there were in Rome twenty monasteries for women, forty for men, and sixty for secular priests living the common life. See S. Beissel, *Die Verehrung der Heiligen und ihrer Reliquien in Deutschland bis zum Beginne des 13. Jahrhunderts (Stimmen aus Maria-Laach*, Supplement No. 47 [Freiburg im Breisgau, 1892]), p. 70 [Tschan's note].

[10] There were guide-books. See reference to Beissel in n. 9 [Tschan's note].

as he pleased. Furthermore, he was not well and the journey
must have taxed his strength. His "sightseeing" was most likely
confined to places he would come across en route to his meetings
and appointments. Otto's palace on the Aventine was close to a
monastery and church built in the seventh century and dedicated
to Saint Boniface. About 970 this institution was assigned to
Greek monks who in the course of time changed the patronage,
and consequently the name, to what it is today—*Sant'Alessio*.
Bernward may have stayed with these monks, for his host, the
emperor, is said to have prepared magnificently for him. On the
Aventine also was the church of *Santa Maria del Priorata*, built
in the ninth century, and not far away the church of *Santa
Sabina*, erected in 425. In the entrance of *Santa Sabina* were
cypress-wood doors adorned with carvings of biblical scenes,
done for the most part in the fifth century. One of them is
perhaps the oldest representation of the crucifixion. It is generally
conceded that these doors inspired the relief-bearing bronze
portals for which Bernward is famous.[11]

The synod to decide Bernward's case against Willigis assembled in the Church of *San Sebastiano*, one of the "Seven Churches
of Rome."[12] Like *Santa Sabina* it is a basilican edifice, but at the
time it was much better known because it stood over one of the
few catacombs open during the Middle Ages.[13] *San Sebastiano*
is on the Appian Way beyond Aurelian's wall. On his way from
the Aventine Bernward would see the *Circus Maximus* but its

---

[11] A. Bertram, *Die Türen von St. Sabina in Rom, das Vorbild der Bern-
wardstüren* (Hildesheim, 1894); H. Grisar, "Kreuz und Kreuzigung auf
der altchristlichen Thüre von S. Sabina in Rom," *Römische Quartalschrift*,
8 (1894), pp. 1–48; and J. J. Berthier, *L'Église de Sainte-Sabine à Rome*
(Freiburg im Breisgau, 1892) [Tschan's note].

[12] The "Seven Churches" are the four patriarchal basilicas St. John
Latern (cathedral and mother church of the world), St. Peter's, St. Paul
Outside the Walls, and Santa Maria Maggiore, plus three other basilicas—
San Lorenzo Outside the Walls, Santa Croce in Gerusalemme, and San
Sebastiano. These are the principal churches visited by pilgrims to Rome.

[13] The word "basilica" literally means "royal" in Greek (the Greek word
for "king" is *basileus*). In Roman times a basilica could be any large
rectangular structure used for a variety of purposes, but in the course of
the Middle Ages the word gradually was confined to Christian churches
with that kind of design.

glories had disappeared when the last race was run there in
Ostrogothic times [under King Totila in A.D. 549]. Farther on
were the Thermae [Baths] of Caracalla [built in A.D. 212] and
the basilican Church *Santi Nereo ed Achilleo* built about 800 by
Leo III.[14]

In January when he went with his hosts to quell the rebellion
in Tivoli [ancient Tibur], Bernward traveled about a region
where many notables of the Empire had estates. Augustus,
Maecenas and Hadrian built villas near this ancient town of
Tibur, but long before Bernward's time these estates had not
been beautiful to look upon.[15] Neglect quickly led to a state of
dilapidation and desolate ruin. More interesting to him, if he
came over the ancient *Via Tiburtina* was *San Lorenzo fuori le
Mura,* erected in the sixth century on the site of an earlier
Constantinian church, another of the "Seven Churches of Rome"
to which pilgrims flocked from all parts of the Latin world.

Except for the fact that Bernward's column was plainly inspired by that of Trajan or of Marcus Aurelius, or possibly
both, it could reasonably be assumed that he did not visit the
heart of classical Rome on or near the Capitoline Hill.[16] If he
did, there was little to see that would make him appreciate Otto's
dreams about resuscitating the ancient empire. The great *Forum*
had already in Roman times been a quarry from which the

[14] It is ironical that the Baths of Caracalla though in ruins are functioning
as an outdoor theater for summer musical productions, whereas Pennsylvania
Station in New York, which was modelled on the Baths, has been torn
down to make way for a larger edifice.

[15] Maecenas (c. 70 B.C.–8 B.C. was a Roman patron of letters, notably
of the poet Horace. Hadrian was emperor from A.D. 117 to 138.

[16] Trajan's Column was dedicated to the emperor in A.D. 113 to com-
memorate his victory over the Dacians, in what is now Rumania. When
Trajan died in 117, his ashes were placed in an urn beneath the column.
The Doric column is nearly 100 feet tall and is made out of marble. There
is a spiral staircase on the interior with 185 steps. A statue of St. Peter was
placed on top of it in 1587, in place of the statue of the emperor. The
column of Marcus Aurelius was inspired by Trajan's. The lower part is
covered with reliefs depicting the emperor's conquest of the Germans A.D.
171–173). The figures of Marcus Aurelius and the Empress Faustina originally stood atop the column, but in 1589 a statue of St. Paul was put in
their place.

marble was taken either to adorn new buildings or to be burned for the lime. What edifices had not been turned to pious purposes were crumbling to ruin. Theodoric the Ostrogoth [Roman Emperor, A.D. 493–526] had made the last effort to restore them nearly five centuries before, and the rubbish which until recent times buried the *Forum* was already beginning to accumulate.

# 6      *Otto III*

*DO. III. 389 (Documents of Otto III, No. 389) grants eight counties in Italy to the Church but, as Percy Schramm points out in his discussion of this deed (p. 133 ff.), it is not a simple transaction. To appreciate the subtleties of the donation, we need to analyze the structure of the document in comparison with other such deeds.*

*The usual document or diploma of this period consisted of two main parts: (1) the protocol, in two sections, which were roughly equivalent to the salutation and complimentary closing of a formal letter. Protocol, a Greek word meaning literally "the first thing glued," was originally the first sheet of a papyrus roll. The opening section is often called the "initial protocol" to distinguish it from the section of the protocol which came at the end of the document. This concluding section was in turn referred to as the "eschatacol" or "last thing glued." (2) In between came the text of the deed, corresponding to the body of a letter.*

*A typical diploma can be divided into twelve parts. The first four belong to the initial protocol; they are (1) the invocation, usually to Christ or to all Three Persons of the Trinity; (2) the intitulation, containing the name and titles of the grantor; (3) the address, consisting not of the place to which the deed is to be sent, but rather to the people themselves who are to receive it; (4) the salutation, which presents the author's wish for health and welfare to the recipient of the deed.*

*The text was divided into five parts: (1) the preamble, a general prologue; (2) the notification, publishing the intent of the deed; (3)*

*the exposition, giving the reasons why the grant needed to be made; (4) the disposition, stating what the grantee is to receive; (5) the final clauses, which guaranteed that the provisions of the donation would be carried out.*

*Finally came the eschatacol in three parts: (1) the date (but many of the documents between the ninth and the twelfth century, including DO. III. 389, are not dated); (2) the appreciation, a short closing like "Amen" or "Thanks be to God"; (3) the authentication. The authentication was further broken down into component parts, which included a seal and a signature or, for illiterate signators, a mark, often a cross. Kings who could not write commonly used a royal monogram, and this custom was subsequently adopted by monarchs who were literate as well as by those who were not.*

*Since the practice of each chancery differed from the others and the practice within each chancery was altered from reign to reign (particularly in the protocol), we can accurately trace the political history of Europe during the Middle Ages if we know the intricacies of diplomatics—the science of deeds and charters. The interpretation of these documents, however, is full of pitfalls. What is said in the text may seem quite straightforward to an untrained reader and altogether devious to an old hand. Thus DO. III. 389 seems to be a munificent bequest by the emperor to his old friend and tutor Pope Sylvester II but, in reality, nothing is being given away in any absolute sense.*

---

### Otto Grants Eight Counties to the Church of St. Peter

[Invocation] In the name of the Holy and Indivisible Trinity. [Intitulation] Otto, Servant of the Apostles and following the will of God the Savior, Emperor Augustus of the Romans. [Exposition] We acknowledge Rome as head of the world, we

SOURCE. Otto III, DO. 389 (diploma of Otto III granting eight counties to the Church in January, 1001, in *Monumenta Germaniae historica, Diplomata regum et imperatorum Germaniae*, Vol. II, Part 2: *Die Urkunden Otto des III.*, ed. Theodor Sickel, 2nd ed. (Berlin: Weidmann, 1957), pp. 818–820; trans. Boyd H. Hill, Jr.

testify that the Roman Church is the mother of all, but
the negligence and stupidity of the popes have for a long
time obscured the titles of its fame. For not only have they
[the popes] sold and traded to the rabble from the Treasury
of St. Peter those things which seem to be outside the city, but
(we do not say this without pain) whatever they had in this our
royal city, they scattered with greater license and gave up both
St. Peter and St. Paul to the common use, money deciding in all
cases; they even despoiled the altars and always introduced disorder in place of reparation. Indeed, the papal laws being con-
fused and the Roman Church being now cast down, certain of
the popes became so aggressive that they joined the greatest
part of our Empire to their Apostolic See, not asking what and
how much they lost by their faults, not caring how much they
squandered by wilful vanity, but since they had dismissed those
areas despoiled by themselves, they turned to the property of
others, that is, to ours, as if casting back their guilt into our
Empire. And these are fabrications invented by themselves, in
which John the Deacon, nicknamed "the one with the mutilated
fingers," wrote a deed in golden letters and fixed the circumstances of the long-standing lie, under the title of Constantine
the Great. These are also fabrications by which they say a certain Charles gave our public goods to St. Peter. To this we
respond that that same Charles could not rightfully give away
anything since he was put to flight by a better Charles, deprived
of the Empire, now destitute and nullified; therefore, he gave
what he did not have; he gave as he doubtless was able to give—
as one who had acquired badly and did not hope to possess it for
long.

[Disposition] Therefore, having disdained these forged deeds
and false writings, we give to St. Peter out of our largesse what
is ours, not what is his, just as if we are conferring our own
property. So for the love of St. Peter we have elected Lord
Sylvester our teacher as our Pope, and God willing we have
ordained and created him most serene. Thus for the love of that
same Lord Pope Sylvester we confer gifts from our property
on St. Peter, so that the teacher may offer on the part of his
pupil something to our prince Peter.

Therefore we, Otto, confer and donate certain counties to St.

Peter for the love of our teacher Lord Pope Sylvester so that he may hold them for the honor of God and St. Peter, with his salvation and ours, and may administer them for the success of his apostolate and our Empire. We concede for his administration: Pesaro, Fano, Senigallia, Ancona, Fossambrone, Cagli, Iesi, and Osimo, so that no one may ever dare to make any trouble for him and St. Peter or disturb him in any way.

[Final Clauses] Whoever presumes to take them away, may he give away all he has and St. Peter receive what is his. So that this may be preserved in eternity by all, we confirm this deed with our victorious hand, so help us God, and we order it to be marked with our seal, so that it may be valid for him [the Pope] and his successors.

[Authentication]

Sign of Lord Otto (Monogram)
most invincible Emperor Augustus
of the Romans.

# SECONDARY WORKS

7 *Geoffrey Barraclough*

*Geoffrey Barraclough, born in 1908, was educated at Oriel College, Oxford, and the University of Munich. He became Professor of Mediaeval History at the University of Liverpool in 1945 and Research Professor of International History at the University of London in 1956. He has also been visiting professor at the University of California, La Jolla, and at Brandeis. Among his many publications are* Public Notaries and the Papal Curia *(1934);* Papal Provisions *(1935);* Mediaeval Germany *(1938);* The Origins of Modern Germany *(1946);* Factors in German History *(1946);* The Mediaeval Empire *(1950); and* History in a Changing World *(1955).*

---

## THE MONARCHY AND ITS RESOURCES

In attempting to reduce the conception of the "stem-duchy" to its proper place in constitutional history we must be careful not to underestimate its political importance. There is no doubt whatever that the tendency to disintegration into four or five racial divisions and the growing concentration of monarchical powers in the hands of local leaders was a serious menace to the Saxon rulers and their main preoccupation. It was, without doubt, a source of political weakness and, until it was overcome, a stumbling block in the path of the monarchy and of royal attempts to establish a stronger monarchical power. There is no

SOURCE. From *Mediaeval Germany 911-1250*, Translations of Essays by German Historians, *Studies in Medieval History*, Volume 1, 1938, Edited by G. Barraclough, by permission of Basil Blackwell, Oxford, pp. 47-73.

doubt, further, that the fact of racial disunity—though no more serious than that of tenth century England—favoured the pretensions of provincial magnates.[1] But the pretensions themselves were political pretensions and could be overcome by political measures: they were due to the weakening of the monarchy in the face of the invasions and irruptions of the ninth century and could be overcome by a reassertion of monarchical powers, provided that the monarchical reaction arrived before the new political forces were firmly anchored in the constitution, endowed with rights and recognized as stable elements in the organization of the realm.

And this, at least, was achieved. The Saxon and Salian kings still had redoubtable political opposition to face; but their prompt action saved them from the far more difficult task of uprooting an established institution. Weak as were the foundations which the East Frankish rulers left for the German kings of the Saxon dynasty, they were strong as compared with the basis on which the wielders of ducal power had to build. The inheritance of the dukes goes back to the dark days of the dying ninth century: the inheritance of the German kings reaches back to the heights of the Frankish monarchy. The German monarchy, indeed, is the Frankish monarchy: Henry I [919–936], on his elevation to the throne, ceases to be a Saxon and passes under Frankish law, adopts the traditions and takes over the powers of the Frankish kings, becomes a Frank. And this Frankish tradition was not, like so much tradition, an empty shell. It meant at the very least that the German monarchy did not have to start anew in 919 on a new foundation. The proceedings at Forchheim, in which Henry I was accepted as king, implied, as Sickel has written, the "maintenance of an existing state," the acceptance of the Frank-

---

[1] A comparison of the position of the German dukes with that of the pre- and post-Conquest earls might prove instructive. Before the twelfth century and the growth of the new forces released by the Investiture Contest, the position of the German dukes was as indefinite as that of the Anglo-Norman earl, to whom no historian would attribute specific constitutional functions. On the other hand, the potentialities of the position which the earls claimed, but failed to substantiate, become more apparent through a comparison with their peers in Germany [Barraclough's note].

ish monarchy.[2] But even more than this was implied. The Frankish kings had welded, however imperfectly, the races they ruled into a unity, and this unity, the *regnum Theutonicorum* [kingdom of the Teutons], was also maintained intact. The Frankish kings, with whom Henry I was now associated, were more than rulers over the Frankish people: their realm was the *regnum Theutonicorum*, and the unity of this realm is an undeniable historical fact. It is characteristic that, at the moment when tribal separatism is supposed to have been flourishing unchecked, Arnulf of Bavaria's object was not to set up a separate Bavarian state—whether duchy or kingdom is of small importance—but to wrest the *regnum Theutonicorum* from Henry.[3] This tacit acceptance of the Frankish heritage by one of those whose ducal strivings were threatening to destroy the work of the Frankish kings is striking testimony that in 919 more than a mere tradition of a monarchy over the German peoples survived. Not merely a nebulous idea of a monarchical overlordship but the traditional royal authority, by whomsoever it might be exercised, was accepted by all parties in 919. "Even if Conrad, Henry and Otto I were kings by election," it has been said, "the election merely determined who was to wield the existing royal authority and was not a reconstitution and conferment of royal authority on the part of supposedly autogenous tribal powers.[4] That the elected ruler was legally considered a Frank

---

[2] Theodor Sickel, professor at the University of Vienna and head of the Institut für Österreichische Geschichtsforschung, became director in 1873 of the *Diplomata* section of the *Monumenta Germaniae historica*. By minute stylistic criticism he was able to ascertain the authors and scribes in various chanceries and to determine the validity of the documents more accurately than ever before. Among other works, he was the author of *Acta regum et imperatorum Karolinorum digesta et enarrata*, 2 vols. (Vienna, 1877–1868).

[3] Arnulf the Bad, Duke of Bavaria (907–937), was a rival claimant to the throne of Germany. Henry I finally obtained his recognition in 921 at Regensburg (Ratisbon), after he had besieged the town, according to Widukind. But Arnulf remained more independent than the other dukes: he kept the privilege of appointing his own bishops; he coined his own money; and he pursued his own foreign policy.

[4] Conrad, Duke of Franconia, German king (911–918), was troubled with revolts by Arnulf of Bavaria and Henry of Saxony, but eventually chose Henry as his successor.

is a clear indication that he was taking over existing powers superior to those of the aristocratic leaders in the various racial divisions—namely, the authority of the Frankish or East Frankish kings. And the solid basis of this royal authority was the unity of the lands over which it was exercised, the fact that the legal conception of an "East Frankish kingdom" corresponded to the vital reality of an indivisible German realm." Only an exaggeration of the stability and permanence of the tribal divisions, only a mistaken conception of the fixity and mature organization of the "stem-duchies" can turn the hard fact of firmly established royal authority into an empty, almost mythical tradition of monarchical rule, handed down from Frankish times. The persons who were calling themselves dukes were, without doubt, the most powerful force of the age, the mightiest group with which the king had to deal. "But this patent fact may be admitted without supposing that, at the beginning of the tenth century, it was an established legal and constitutional belief that a king and a kingdom could only be created by a sort of contract with the duchies which, in this view, were the real states at the beginning of German history and could alone establish a state above themselves. However important the dukes may have been, there still existed, in the traditions of the church and in Frankish tradition, a consciousness of the unity of the continental races outside the West Frankish limits. It is not necessary to exaggerate the Frankish character of the German kingdom in order to recognize that—above all, at the moment of transition from a Frankish to a German kingdom—the handing over of royal authority by the Frankish folk was more important than the consent of the 'stem-duchies'."[5]

It is out of the question for us to consider here in detail either the legal character or the development of the German monarchy. What we have already said is a sufficient indication that it was not limited, at the beginning of its history, by specific organized tribal institutions which, if they had existed, would have placed it in a different and less fortunate position than the monarchy

[5] Heinrich Heimpl, *Bemerkungen zur Geschichte König Heinrichs des Ersten* (Sächsische Akademie der Wissenschaften, Philosophisch-historische Klasse, 1937), p. 30.

in France or England. It is well, also, to see, as the work of
Heimpel has shown, that the transference of authority from
Frank to Saxon, the accession of a new dynasty to the Frankish
inheritance, was achieved by a process of "designation" which
was the work of the Franks alone, acting in the person of their
leader, Eberhard.[6] The change of dynasty, therefore, was not
made the occasion for the assertion of novel electoral principles:
no precedent was created which might have bound the monarchy in the future, no step was taken which radically differen-
tiated the German monarchy from the West Frankish. It is true
that, as time passes, the contrast between election and hereditary
succession becomes prominent in German history; but there is
nothing specifically German in this antithesis, which is best
understood when considered—as Kern has considered it—in its
broad European setting.[7] Blood-right, election and consecration
were the primary constituents of royal authority in all the states
of mediaeval Europe. If in thirteenth century Germany the
electoral element was predominant, this was the result of a long
historical development, and not a permanent fact which had
dominated the German position from the very beginning. Moreover we must not forget the radical transformation which the
idea of "election" underwent in this period of three hundred
years. "Election" in the tenth century, so far as we can define
its content, was never more than "choice" in the broadest sense,
and usually no more than "assent". *Laudatio* or *collaudatio*
[approval] expresses the meaning of the legal act better than
*electio:* "acclamation" is the people's share in the making of
its ruler, and "election" in the sense of "choice" or "designation" of his successor normally falls to the reigning king himself.
But even if we use the word "election" in a strict mediaeval
sense, we shall be wrong if we presuppose an antithesis between
election and hereditary right: they are rather two different ways

[6] Eberhard was Duke of Franconia (918–939) and brother of Conrad I.
It was Eberhard who in 919 took the royal insignia to Henry of Saxony
after the death of Conrad, thereby waiving his own claims to the throne.
[7] Fritz Kern is author of *Gottesgnadentum und Widerstandsrecht im
früheren Mittelalter* (1914), trans. S. B. Chrimes as *Kingship and Law in
the Middle Ages* (New York: Frederick A. Praeger, 1956), Vol. IV of
*Studies in Mediaeval History*, ed. Geoffrey Barraclough.

of revealing what is right and what must rightly be, and a third way is added when, with the accession of Otto I, consecration becomes an essential element in the making of a German king. The unity of this threefold revelation of God's will, it has been said, is characteristic of the Ottonian age, its destruction marks the beginning of a new era; but even in the twelfth century, it may be noted, the ideal of a harmonious cooperation of the three elements remains alive . . . .

The "coronation order" which seems to have been composed in Mainz for the elevation of Otto II in 961, and which closely follows the ceremony devised for the coronation of Otto I in 936, is the best expression of the tenth century conception of the German monarchy. The terms *electio* [election], *eligere* [to elect], although they had appeared in the models on which the [Mainz] *ordo* was based, were carefully avoided, and no binding promise was imposed, as in France, on the new king.[8] All the emphasis falls, on the contrary, on hereditary right and on divine right. The king is Christ's vicar, "cuius nomen vicemque gestare crederis" [whose name and office you are believed to bear"]: Christ has appointed him to be "mediator" between clergy and people: his "regnum" [kingdom] is "a Deo concessum" [granted by God]. But God has delegated the throne to his appointed by hereditary right: he holds it by "paternal succession". And this statement is no theory or courtier's doctrine, but a recognition of existing fact. Otto the Great had gone beyond the old, well-established right of "designating" his successor, and had had his son, Otto II, raised to the throne as co-ruler in 961, and even after Otto I's death in 973 it was from 961 that Otto II's regnal years ran. In the same way Henry III's regnal year [1039] began with the death of his father and not with his own coronation. These facts, and still more the minority rule of Otto III and Henry IV [1056–1065] and the regencies of royal mothers, illustrate the firm establishment of the hereditary principle. In the whole period from 911 to 1254 the right of the king's son to succeed, the right of the father to nominate a son as successor, was an accepted axiom of public law; and since

[8] But compare Widukind's account of Otto's royal coronation: "If this election pleases you, signify by raising your right hand."

election conferred the royal dignity on the whole dynasty and not merely on the single ruler, the succession of a new king from the old line was a matter solely for the royal house to decide and not the business of princes or people. There was, indeed, no question of excluding "election", for the king who was no despot desired the acclamation and support of his *curia* [court]; but in the circumstances which obtained "election" could only signify assent, affirmation of the royal proposal, in the same way as the *concilium regis* [council of the king] was called on to assent to questions of peace and war and public policy. Rejection of the king's proposal, a demand for reconsideration, is conceivable, but not an "election" in the modern sense of the term, not a "free election", for the magnates consulted had no alternative to "electing" the king's son.

The situation was, of course, radically different when there was no direct successor from the royal house, as (for example) after the death of Otto III in 1002. A new royal house had then to be chosen, and it is clear that, in such a situation, there was always the possibility of an *electio libera* [free election]. For this reason great emphasis has always been laid on the rapid extinction of the German royal dynasties, on the fate which prevented one long line of rulers consolidating its position, like the Capetian house in France. But the fact is that, for the first two centuries of German history, the so-called "free elections" are the most striking proof of the strength of hereditary principles. Henry II [1002–1024] was elected as the successor to the Saxon inheritance: the sole basis of his candidature was his hereditary right. In 1034 the only two candidates who were considered both claimed as descendants of Otto I's daughter, Liutgard, and Conrad II [1024–1039] succeeded to no small degree, on the one hand, because of the Carolingian blood in the veins of his wife, Gisela, and on the other, because Henry II's widow, Kunigunde, handed him the royal insignia and thus "designated" him as the candidate best qualified to succeed. Even after the revolutionary storms of the last years of the eleventh century the belief in hereditary right is still a part of the common German inheritance. Lothar III [1125–1137] was, in the last analysis, only an anti-king set up in opposition to the legitimate heirs, his election was the last of the revolutionary acts

which had torn Germany under Henry IV [1056–1106]; but
even he could emphasize claims of blood, and after his death
the traditional attitude was once again predominant. The princes
[Lothar and Welf]⁹ . . . could not tolerate a king without royal
blood in his veins . . . and so they set up Conrad III [1137–
1152], a man of royal birth. Far from the extinction of the ruling
dynasty being the sign for a consolidation of supposed electoral
"rights", nothing is more remarkable than the disinclination to
use this opportunity for strengthening particularist claims and
princely pretensions. Instead of building up a right of free choice,
the princes seem mainly concerned, on such occasions, in
genuinely discriminating between the reasonable claims of
junior branches of the royal house. It is characteristic that the
opportunities for princely egotism which such events as the
death of Otto III presented, were allowed to pass if not altogether
without exploitation at all events without any direct attempt
to weaken the position of the monarchy, and that when a
real attempt was made to put electoral principles into play in
1077, it was part of a revolutionary programme.¹⁰ The conception of real "election" arises, in short, not as the result of the
lack of direct heirs, not because Germany frequently found
itself without an acknowledged successor, but as an explicit
breach of tradition in circumstances which were revolutionary.
Instead of exploiting the occasions presented by the death of a
childless king, the princes manufactured an occasion when the
time was ripe. This fact, which is rarely observed, is a striking
indication that the growth of the electoral principle in Germany

⁹ The Welfs were dukes of Bavaria and later, by marriage, also dukes of
Saxony. Frederick I Barbarossa (1152–1190) was a Welf on his mother's
side. It is the name of this noble house that came into Italian as Guelph.
The Guelphs were regarded as the enemies of the Hohenstaufen, one of
whose possessions—Waiblingen—gave the name Ghibellines to the Hohenstaufen faction in the Italian cities.

¹⁰ In 1077, during the investiture controversy, Henry IV in an effort to
save his throne went to Canossa in northern Italy where Gregory VII
(1073–1085) was visiting Countess Mathilda of Tuscany, a powerful ally of
the pope. Henry supposedly stood in the snow for three days until the
pope granted him an audience and heard the emperor's request for for-
giveness. Eventually Henry was absolved, and the pope gave up plans to
elect a new king in Germany.

is due, not to the undermining of hereditary principles by frequent changes of dynasty, but to the growth of new ideas and of a new outlook. It is not our business, at the moment, to explain or discuss this new atmosphere which sprang from a novel combination of ancient Germanic and clerical conceptions of the right to resist constituted authority, and which was, historically, an answer to the centralizing policy of the Salian kings with its inevitable hostility to ancient law and popular custom. For us the essential fact is to see the revolutionary nature of the electoral claim enunciated at Forchheim in 1077. It was not the culmination of a gradual process, but a breach of tradition, a denial of current practice, and an attempt to sever continuity with the past. In the cleft were planted the seeds of a new age.

But it has been acutely remarked that the Investiture Contest, though it may have been the occasion for the definition and consolidation of clerical and princely claims, was equally the occasion for a definition and strengthening of monarchical ideas, that the new emphasis on electoral rights necessarily produced its reaction, a heightened belief in the monarchy and in monarchical rights. We have been warned against regarding the election of [Lothar III in] 1125 as a final victory for the principle of "free election", and Joachimsen has rightly pointed out that, important as the Investiture Contest was in German constitutional development, its importance did not lie in the transference of emphasis from heredity to election: "the view that the German kingdom was an elective monarchy," he says, "did not become finally prevalent until some two centuries after the election of Rudolf of Rheinfelden."[11] It was only in the

---

[11] Paul Joachimsen, "The Investiture Contest and the German Constitution," trans. Geoffrey Barraclough in *Studies in Mediaeval History*, II, p. 127. (The article originally appeared as "Der Investiturstreit und die deutsche Verfassung," in *Bayerische Blätter für das Gymnasialschulwesen*, LVIII [1922], pp. 53-75.)

Rudolf of Rheinfelden, a Burgundian count, became Duke of Swabia in 1057 and was elected King of Germany during the same year that Henry IV went to Canossa (January, 1077) and received absolution from Gregory VII. The German nobles were taken aback by the pope's action but nevertheless held a diet at Forchheim in Bavaria in March at which they elected Rudolf king. Although the pope did not attend, he recognized the claims of both kings. He remained neutral for three years and then in 1080 excom-

thirteenth century—under the stress of very different circumstances—that election became the decisive element in the making of a German king. It is true, indeed, that the old feeling of stability and solidity is lacking in the twelfth century. . . . although succession by primogeniture was possible at all three elections subsequent to the death of Conrad III in 1152, the eldest son was on no occasion chosen, but [there is] new emphasis . . . placed on the electoral rights of the princes. . . . Perhaps it is not far-fetched to attribute this change of emphasis to Henry V's break with his father's policy, and his attempt to cooperate with the nobility. Nevertheless the hereditary principle was adequately safeguarded in so far as the new king was, in each case, taken from the *stirps regia* [royal stock]; and when Henry VI, who, elected in 1167, had been co-regent since 1184 and sole ruler after Barbarossa went on crusade, succeeded in 1190 and dispensed with re-election, the chroniclers were not wrong in maintaining that he followed "quasi successione hereditaria" [as if by hereditary succession].

Even after the Investiture Contest, therefore, and in spite of the constitutional transformations of the twelfth century . . . the hereditary principle was vigorous and—by 1190—predominant. Before the revolution under Henry IV, on the other hand, there had been no question at all of "election" in the sense in which the term is used to-day. Once again it is worth emphasizing that, under the Ottonian and Salian rulers, blood-right and election were the opposite of antitheses. In West Francia election, oaths, consecration, coronation, investiture and other formalities had been piled together, a mass of uncoordinated forms and acts, with the object of strengthening weak and disputed claims—an agglomeration which was a confession of legal hesitancy and uncertainty, a vain attempt to counter treason and faithlessness. In Germany the same acts and forms, organically combined, were a testimony to a high consciousness of legality and of the strength derived from strict legality. Native Germanic tradition, feudal practice, Christian belief, each demanded consideration,

---

municated Henry, deposed him, and set up Rudolf as his lawful successor. But Rudolf died in battle the same year, and Henry remained in control in spite of papal opposition.

each had its place: because each of the three factors was a constituent element in constitutional life none could be ignored without injury to established right. "With these facts in mind we can understand the juxtaposition, so characteristic of Ottonian times, of factors which were later to become exclusive antitheses. The father's will, the electors' will, God's will; enthronement by laity and clergy; hereditary right, election, divine right; anointment, spiritual investiture, coronation, the symbolic feast—how many heterogenous traditions are here fused together! How many elements supplement and strengthen each other which after the Investiture Contest will be played off the one against the other! Such fusion is not the result of hesitancy, not incompetence of constitutional thought, but a reflection of the first happy day in German history—the day on which princes, clergy and people joined together under divine guidance in favour of one monarch and the monarch himself asserted unchallenged every right to which a ruler in that age could lay claim, on which he received every symbolic and religious assurance which the century knew."[12]

If we take our stand at the coronation of Henry III in 1028, eleven years before his father's death, we can only wonder at the strength of the German monarchy. Compared with the France of Robert II [996–1031] it was a homogenous land, held together by solid traditions, ruled by energetic and intelligent sovereigns. The leadership of Europe was firmly established in German hands. Nor was this power and predominance based on weak foundations. The Ottonian and Salian emperors were not merely holding down the cowed but ultimately invincible forces of particularism and princely egotism. The weaknesses which are so often alleged to have been eating away the roots of the monarchical tree were non-existent. The "stem-duchy" . . . never developed into a constitutional actuality. The crown was not beset by a destructive conception of electoral monarchy. It is true that Germany in 919, like every other country in Europe, still needed welding more firmly together; but this was not on

[12] P. E. Schramm, "Die Krönung in Deutschland bis zum Beginn des Salischen Hauses," *Zeitschrift der Savigny-Stiftung für Rechtsgeschichte, Kanonistische Abteilung*, XXIV (1935), pp. 213–214.

account of a unique tribal organization, strongly resistant to centralization, but because, like every other country in Europe, the dominions subject to the German king has suffered the ravages of invasion from north and east. Nowhere else, however, had the monarchy shown itself more competent to resist and counteract the resultant disintegration . . . more important and more effective [than its political measures] was what we may broadly call its "cultural" policy. A constant interchange of personalities broke down local bounds and local feeling. Already under Otto I a monk of Reichenau became abbot of St. Maurice in Magdeburg and subsequently bishop of Hildesheim, while the Saxon Hildeward received at St. Gallen the education which he was later to convert to good account in Saxony as bishop of Halberstadt. Regensburg became a connecting link between north and south: Bamberg, the bishopric created by Henry II, was as important culturally as politically. The zeal and fervour embodied in the German reform movements of the eleventh century—movements which, influenced though they may have been by Cluniac inspiration, quickly developed along independent lines and produced specifically German fruits from roots growing deep in German soil—were used by Henry II and Henry III to bind the land together, and under Henry IV the Hirsau congregation performed the same task. By the time of Henry II cultural interchanges between north and south were so frequent and normal that the citation of examples would give a false impression: it was no longer a question of isolated personalities but of a broad and solid movement. As the eleventh century proceeded regional differences gradually fell into the background: it was then that the collective name for the German people, *Teutonici*, rapidly became usual. Even the Saxons who rose in rebellion "pro libertate, pro legibus, pro patria sua" [for liberty, for laws, for their own country] in 1073, showed no inclination to resist the rule of Conrad II and Henry III or to stand apart, under the first two Salian kings, from the rest of Germany. By the middle of the eleventh century the realm was firmly united under its ruling dynasty and all traces of particularism seemed dead.

The unity and solidarity under the crown which is apparent

at the middle of the eleventh century was due, as is well known, in a special degree to the co-operation of leading churchmen and the harmonious relations between church and crown. But if the fact is well known, it remains true that there is scarcely any chapter of German history which is so little understood as the relations of crown and church before the Investiture Contest. In England and elsewhere where Ulrich Stutz's thorough studies of pre-Gregorian ecclesiastical institutions have never been sufficiently appreciated, these relationships are still seen through partisan Hildebrandine eyes, the Gregorian thesis that the royal position in the church was built on usurpation and violence is still too unhesitatingly adopted.[13] We have to realize, in the first place, that before the creation of a Roman canon law there was a consistent body of Germanic canon law, accepted by all parties, which took a very different attitude from later legislation both to the laity and to the rights of the laity in the church, and the essential element of this Germanic law was the proprietary right of the lord over the churches he had founded and over their lands. It is this paramount overlordship, and not the strong hand of irreligious monarchs, which explains the interference of German rulers in the internal administration of the German church during the tenth and eleventh centuries. They are exercising a right, not abusing a power. But they are also performing a duty. For we have to realize, in the second place, that the king was no mere layman. By his consecration—which had all the significance of a sacrament until, at the earliest, the middle of the twelfth century—he was constituted *rex et sacerdos* [king and priest], and his sacerdotal position not only made him, as we have seen, the chosen mediator between clergy and people, but also imposed on him the duty of "ruling" his church. Thus Henry III could reply to a radical bishop: "Ego vero similiter sacro oleo data mihi prae caeteris imperandi potestate sum perunctus [I am anointed with the power of ruling given to me before others just as I am anointed with holy oil]." To regard the relations of church and state in tenth and eleventh century Germany as an "alliance" against the lay princes is therefore a

---

[13] Hildebrand became Pope Gregory VII (1073-1085).

falsification. The king did not need to ally with a church which was tied to him by proprietary and sacerdotal bonds: it was his church and he was its divinely appointed ruler.

The German monarch could therefore use the church, not as an unwilling tool diverted from its proper function, but as an instrument placed by God in royal hands for the work of civilization and social organization, regarding the objects of which church and state were still as one. It is often stated that ecclesiastical co-operation was only obtained at a great price, at a cost which ultimately ruined the monarchy. The immediate political advantage of Henry II's creation of Bamberg and Henry III's support of Bremen, for example, is obvious enough and does not fail to win recognition, but the king, it is said, was only raising up powers which were bound, in the end, to turn against himself or his successors. Against this view, however, it must be insisted—even at the risk of stating the obvious—that no king in the first half of the eleventh century could foresee the attack which was to be made in the next generation on what, for three hundred years and more, had been unquestioningly accepted as the rightful and firmly established relationship of church and state. It could not be foreseen that the state's paramount ownership of the lands of the "national church" would be called in question, and that the direct administrative control, which was the corollary of such ownership, would be transformed, after the Concordat of Worms [1122], into an indirect feudal overlordship. But the tendency to apply Hildebrandine ideas to an age in which they had no following is not the only reason why the Ottonian and Salian kings are supposed to have sacrificed their ultimate prospects to their more immediate advantage. More significant still, is a radically mistaken conception of the connected institutions of "immunity" and "advocacy". If the immunity, which played so large a part in German governmental organization in the middle ages, was simply exemption from state control, and if the advocate was an official of the immune church, who took the place of the count and was responsible to the church as the count was responsible to the king, it is obvious that the creation of immunities on a large scale—and this fact stands altogether beyond dispute— must rapidly lead to a dislocation and disintegration of government. But neither supposition is true. It is essential in the first place to understand that—in this regard as in others—the mediaeval German constitution and its specific institutions were anything but a direct, unaltered continuation of the Frankish or Carolingian constitution. Whatever the Frankish advocate may have been, the theory that the advocate was an "official" of the church which he represented, only entered German history with the growth of the reform movement in the eleventh century, and was not really successful—so far as it was successful at all—until the thirteenth century. In the earlier period the advocate is a lord, exercising lordly powers over the church's dependents closely connected, if not identical, with the proprietary rights, which the proprietary lord possessed in the church's lands. The immunity, also, is not the *emunitas* which had found its way from Roman into Merovingian institutions. The charters themselves use other less antiquarian terms, *defensio, tuitio, mundeburdium,* to describe the institution, and *mundeburdium*—the special protection and authority exercised by a lord over his household and his household dependents—is the essence of the institution, as it develops after the accession of Louis the Pious in 813. A grant of "immunity" to a church or monastery, therefore, means its inclusion in the household of the king, implies that it shares the special protection and the special relationship with the crown with which the royal household was favoured. Far from loosening the ties between the monarchy and the churches, immunity created a new bond, stronger than the ordinary administrative connexion: it "exempted" churches from the ordinary county administration, but only in order to place them under the more direct authority, the *mundeburdium,* of the king. And this was the sense and purpose of the whole institution. Threatened in the first half of the tenth century by the possibility of the growth of a regional or "tribal" church organization, the monarchy bound the churches of the realm to itself by the "immunity" and thus acquired a new means of unifying the realm. Possessed of the *mundeburdium,* the king had the right to appoint or to participate in the appointment of bishops and abbots, and the result was the appointment of bishops who had graduated through the royal chapel and were imbued with the same conscientious spirit as Henry II himself. Pos-

sessed of the *mundeburdium*, the king was himself the supreme
advocate of the imperial churches, and the local advocates who
performed the actual duties of the office were only his subordinates and representatives. Even where the right to "elect" the
local advocate was granted to a monastery or bishopric, the
king, as supreme advocate, retained the right to "constitute"
him in office—his authority, in other words, derived from the
crown, and the king maintained control, for *electio* was a preliminary, *constitutio* the decisive stage in appointment.

These ideas applied from the beginning to the churches of
which the monarchy was founder and over which it therefore
exercised proprietary rights. But as the proprietary régime gradually gained ground and was applied, as the prevailing system,
to churches which had come into the king's hands in other ways,
the ideas that went with it were extended also, and by the time
of Henry II the ancient bishoprics were treated as standing under
the royal *mundeburdium* and subject to the king's advocacy.
Thus the organization of all churches directly dependent on the
crown was consolidated, and at the same time the attempt was
made to extend the bounds of the "royal" or "imperial" or
"national" church, until all the churches of the realm were united
in one body. This was the ultimate meaning of the numerous
concessions of immunity to churches founded by the lay nobility: a grant of immunity and protection and freedom meant
that immunity, that protection and that freedom which was assured by membership of the *Reichskirche*, the "national church"
—it signified the end of the proprietary rights of the lay lord
and incorporation in the great ecclesiastical body which the king
alone ruled. Nor was the laity in ignorance of this intention:
"regalem nolui facere, nisi coactus [I was unwilling to make it
royal unless coerced]," wrote Ulrich of Lenzburg in 1036, but
he could not withstand the dual pressure of the crown, striving
to unite the German church, and of the canons, seeking the
*libertas* which the crown alone could give, and by 1045 his
family foundation of Beromünster had become a royal priory.
Thus the monarchy in the eleventh century was gradually welding together a united German church and—more than this—
a united imperial church, immunity and advocacy were being
extended until they comprehended the whole ecclesiastical orga-

nization of the empire from the Holy See to the smallest monastery. Closely attached to the royal household and through the
household to the king himself, under the control of the supreme
royal advocate—a control reaffirmed, for all who were spiritually
minded, by the king's sacerdotal character—the church was
more firmly attached to the monarchy than ever before. Immunity and advocacy, in short, had proved their value as centralizing forces, as institutions which were building up the
resources of the central government and increasing the crown's
hold over the land.

But it would not be correct to regard the strength of the
Ottonian and Salian monarchy as based exclusively on the
church and on the fidelity and good-will of the bishops. It is
easy, but it is false to say that the crown relied solely on the
prelates and that when they deserted it—whether the king could
have foreseen the desertion, hardly matters from this point of
view—it had no other resources on which to draw. On the
contrary, the development of the organs of central government
begins very markedly under Otto I. There was, of course, no
separately organized chancery at this period; but the reorganization which succeeded the rebellion of 953-955 brought a
new consistency and vigour into the routine of government.
The supreme office of *archicapellanus*, the control of the whole
clerical staff of the royal household, which in the previous
half-century had been disputed between Mainz, Cologne, Trier
and Salzburg, passed to Otto's brother, Bruno, the archbishop of
Cologne, and to his son, William, the archbishop of Mainz, and
on Bruno's death in 965, was permanently attached to the see of
Mainz. At the same time a new permanent official, the *cancel-
larius*, was placed in charge of the clerical work, responsible to
the *archicapellanus* and controlling the clerks engaged in the
written work of government. But most important of all is the
sudden increase in the number of notaries or clerks. From
the beginning of Henry I's reign until 956 only one or two
clerks seem to have been deputed at one time to carry out the
writing of charters: in 956 the number suddenly rises to as many
as eight, and all were men who performed a long period of
service. This change reflects the growth of settled government
and the increasing activity of the monarchy. Permanence of

machinery—expressed particularly in the establishment of the office of chancellor—meant permanence and continuity of governmental tradition.

The development of local administration came later, but was no less significant of the constructive powers of the monarchy. Its main feature was the development of the *ministerialis* class as the nucleus of a royal bureaucracy. [In] the great administrative programme of the Salian period [Conrad II, 1024–39, to Henry V, 1106–1125], two essential points were centralization of government in Goslar and the revindication and closer organization and exploitation of the crown lands, but the key to the whole was the building up of a ministerial bureaucracy, which could be trusted to put the programme into effect. This use of the ministerial class, however, is only one side of the general tendency of the Salian rulers to draw away from the nobility —the small group of freeborn men in whose hands long tradition had placed the sum of governmental power—and make contact with the unfree but socially and economically rising classes, the peasants and the townspeople. It was no accident of history that the Rhenish towns were among the staunchest supporters of Henry IV throughout the rebellions of his reign, or that the *Landfrieden* of 1103 gave special attention to the legal position of the servile peasant class.[14] It is true that, in all this process, only a beginning was made during the period between Henry II and Henry IV; but that beginning is enough to show the vitality of the monarchy and its ability to adapt itself to new social conditions. It is essential to insist on this fact, which we have also observed in the development of immunity and advocacy and of the *Eigenkirchenwesen* [proprietary church], because it is still too often stated that the government of the Saxons and Salians was simply a restoration of the Carolingian régime, a pure reaction, antiquarian in spirit, sterile, lacking in original power, incapable of development. That this view overrates the durability of Carolingian institutions, and particularly of the county sys-

---

[14] The Land Peace or Imperial Peace of 1103 was declared by Henry IV in Mainz for four years. The penalties for serious crimes were extended to the propertied classes, who up to then had been able to dodge them by payment of wergild.

tem, goes without saying; but it also underrates the vigour and spontaneity of German public life in the tenth and eleventh centuries, and particularly the vitality incorporated in the monarchy. Far from representing a period in which an obsolescent system was sinking into decay, the age of Henry II, Conrad II and Henry III sees the monarchy already grasping at the opportunities which the rise of new classes to political importance was creating. It was already on the path which fifty years and more later the Norman rulers were to tread in England, and which the Capetians were hardly to reach before the second half of the twelfth century.

## 8                    *Martin Lintzel*

*Martin Lintzel (1901–1955) was associate professor at Kiel and, subsequently, at Halle where he was promoted to professor of medieval and modern history in 1942. He was a member of the Saxon Academy of Sciences (Leipzig).* His publications include: Studien über Liudprand von Cremona *(1933);* Karl der Grosse und Widukind *(1935);* Die Anfänge des deutschen Reiches *(1942); and* Die Kaiserpolitik Ottos des Grossen *(1943). Lintzel's copious bibliography includes works that do not deal with history, such as a monograph about love and death in the works of the poet Heinrich von Kleist and twelve plays of his own, one of which is a tragicomedy called* The Divine Orpheus *and another, in blank verse,* The Trojan Horse. *Between 1937 and 1955 Lintzel directed twenty-four dissertations, most of them dealing with the tenth century.*

---

### THE IMPERIAL POLICY OF OTTO THE GREAT

. . . The view that universal traditions and concepts in the tenth century compelled the German king toward an imperial

SOURCE. Martin Lintzel "Die Kaiserpolitik Ottos des Grossen," in *Ausgewählte Schriften*, 2 vols. (Berlin: Akademie-Verlag, 1961), II, pp. 201–208, trans. Boyd H. Hill, Jr. Reprinted by permission of the publisher. Plate 11 shows the imperial crown.

PLATE XI.   Imperial crown of Otto I (Kunsthistorisches Museum, Vienna
—Art Reference Bureau).

policy is not correct. To be sure, these traditions were present
and they may have had a certain effect, but it was insignificant.
Neither the eschatological expectations of the time nor the tradition of the Roman or the Carolingian Empire nor even the
model of Charles the Great was powerful enough to force the
statesmen of the tenth century toward an Italian policy, and one
can clearly see that Otto's actions were not decisively determined by such ideological considerations. Likewise it cannot be
proven that the imperial policy arose from the need to secure
the German state both from internal and external foes. That the
rule of the German king over Rome and the Pope was calculated to raise his reputation in the world and his authority over
the German bishops need not be argued. While the acquisition
of northern Italy made impossible an Italian policy of the south
German stem-duchies which would destroy the German feder-
ation, it also prevented any other non-German power from interference in Italy. However, the position of the German king
vis-à-vis his own bishops and the rest of the world was not dependent upon his sovereignty over Rome and the papal curia, and
an Italian policy of the South German stem-duchies could have
been forestalled even if the German king did not go to Pavia.
Had this step not been taken, the encroachment of other powers
on Italy was not to be expected, and we cannot speak of a
threat [to Germany] from the South. Above all the assertion that
Otto considered sovereignty over Rome necessary for the success of his policy in the east is not true. And still less can it be
argued that sovereignty over Rome was needed to justify his
reaching beyond Rome to the South and his policy toward the
Greeks [in Southern Italy]. On the other hand, it is hard to say to
what extent the king's long absences from Germany weakened
the power of the crown. We must admit the possibility that in
Saxony at least this was the case, and it can be asserted that the
imperial policy sapped the strength of the policy in the east
and north, thereby damaging the German position in these territories.

In a word, it might be said that Otto's imperial policy was
not necessary for the internal and external security of the German nation, that it injured various facets of the king's internal

political position, and that it most probably also injured the German policy in the east and north.

This judgment looks at first glance like a condemnation of Otto the Great and his policy, but does it really amount to that? It has often been stressed in the discussion of imperial policy that one must distinguish between the results of this policy and the "guilt" of the man who made it. Even if the imperial policy did damage the German nation, Otto need not be condemned on that account.

One should not measure his actions in terms of benefits or injuries to the nation since, wholly apart from the fact that the state of the tenth century was still embryonic, the interest of the state could not at that time have been the guide-line for the king's decisions. The king, so they say, was less of a politician and statesman than a hero. What he did was determined far more by the heroic, chivalric, and probably also the pious, religious views of the time than by the demands of *raison d'état*. Otto should be compared with the adventuresome Viking chieftains who considered their own folk and state insignificant but who regarded fame, glory, power, and riches as everything. If Otto is judged only by his usefulness to the German state and German people, he is being criticized on the basis of anachronistic standards and would therefore not be treated fairly.

There is doubtless a grain of truth in this point of view: Otto's personality and policy are made into abstractions if he is seen only as a "statesman." But on the other hand, can Otto be entirely explained and justified as a "hero"? If the peoples of the tenth century allowed their kings to be heroes, then they would have suspected those individual monarchs who were not heroic. We know that Hincmar of Reims criticized Charles the Bald for heroics when he undertook his trip to Italy . . . the right of a king to the role of hero had certain limitations in the interest of his state and his people, i.e., his nobles. It might have been easier for a king whose realm was in order to go in search of adventure than for the king of a disturbed country. Just so the German king in the tenth century might have been in a better position for adventure than the king of France.

To give an extreme example, what would the world and the German people have said if their king took it into his head to fight against the Saracens in Spain or to go on a pilgrimage to Jerusalem that would last for several years, as a Norman or a minor German noble might have done? To put it more concretely: if the German counts and bishops needed their king against the dukes, or if the counts along the Saxon border and the missionaries needed him against the Slavs, they would have choked on the idea that it was more glorious for a hero to protect the portals of the Apostles and to fight the emperor of the Greeks than to put down the German dukes and to conquer the Slavs. Indeed, we have seen that Otto's policy by no means met with approval everywhere: his intervention in Italy as well as the imperial coronation in Rome appear to have met with particular disfavor in Germany. Even from the point of view of the tenth century it would be difficult to justify everything on the basis that Otto was a hero.

Although this may be the most appropriate yardstick for the evaluation of Otto, we do not need to concern ourselves about whether Otto was "guilty" according to the standards of his time—and that of course is the only way that one might judge him. We are merely questioning whether it is correct or not (as advanced by scholars of the last century) that Otto's Italian policy was advantageous and necessary both within Germany and on the eastern border. It is this assertion alone that we deny. But with this denial, we have by no means exhausted the possibility of judging Otto's policy even from the purely political and national point of view. In the dispute over imperial policy, most people have taken sides wholly for or wholly against it and have sought either to justify it or to condemn it in every respect.

But one need not view the matter in such a unilateral way: it is much more likely that it had several sides and that if it was harmful in some respects, it was advantageous in others, and perhaps this advantage might have outweighed the harm.

Even if it could be shown that the Italian policy was detrimental to the policy in the east and north (apart from the fact of whether it had harmful consequences internally), we would still not have condemned Ottonian expansion in the south. The modern critic is inclined to do this, for the land east of the Elbe is more important to him than the land south of the Alps, and the Elbe policy seems more national, German, and expedient to him than a policy involving the Po. But did it seem so in the tenth century, and could it be seen from the point of view of the state at the time? For the Saxon count who fought on the Havel and the Spree and for the missionary who sought to extend Christianity there, what took place in these regions might have had greater significance than what happened on the other side of the Alps. But for the counts and bishops of southern Germany the situation would have been reversed; indeed, it might be said that it was easier to lead the Saxons to Italy, than to lead the Swabians or the Bavarians against the Slavs along the Elbe and the Oder. Admittedly to Otto as Saxon duke events on the Saxon frontier must have been more immediate than those on the border of the Alps, but for the German king things were otherwise.

German policy could not make uniform allowances for all borders nor please all interests everywhere. A choice had to be made in favor of whatever was more important, while the less important was set aside. However, from the standpoint of pan-German affairs in the tenth century the Italian policy was more important than the policy toward the Slavs (in spite of all the reservations we have made), and the Saxon house, whose duke had become the German king, had to reckon with the fact that the border policy was being neglected.

There were various reasons why the Italian policy was favored over the policy toward the Slavs in the tenth century. . . . Although the eschatological expectations and the universal traditions and tendencies of the time did not force the German king to go to Pavia, nevertheless the road there was paved with these concepts (even if to a more limited degree than has often been assumed). And if the German king did not need to control the Pope and Italy in order either to run the German church and proselytize the East or to secure German hegemony in Europe, the power and glory of his position was nevertheless enhanced by his authority over Rome and Italy. If he was not obliged to meddle in Italy in order to keep the south German noble houses in the imperial union, this interference still had the effect of securely establishing the king's foreign policy there. And finally it may be said that since there was a certain amount of opposition to the Italian policy, it may be assumed that renunciation of that policy would have encountered at least as much opposition. And if there were circles that presumably wanted an autonomous empire instead of the Roman Empire, there were certainly others that considered the imperial crown won in Rome more glorious and politically expedient.

Apart from this, however, there were still considerations that made the conquest of Lombardy seem more immediate and advantageous than that of the Slavic East. At one time—in contrast with today—expansion into northern Italy was more natural from the standpoint of population than expansion toward the east. The Germans thought of the Slavs as almost totally strange barbarians with a foreign language, foreign religion, and culture, with whom there were virtually no connections. But [the Germans] were related to the Lombard nobles of Italy. In spite of all divisive moments, there was a certain union of interests between the German and the Italian noble houses, which is clearly visible in the works of Liudprand of Cremona. There were numerous cultural ties; they could talk with each other, at least via Latin, and be readily understood; and they professed the same religion and belonged to the same church. The points of opposition between the Germans and the North Italians cannot and should not be denied; yet it must be said that the two people formed a large, relatively close union in contradistinction to the Slavs. Whoever came to Italy came to a land that was always a neighbor; whoever came to the Slavs came to strangers.

More important still perhaps for an aggressive foreign policy was the fact that the land of the Slavs was poor, whereas Italy was rich. To be sure, the territories of the Slavs were not totally unproductive economically. We know that the Germans had trade relations with the east; and the strong interest that the Vikings showed for the Slavic lands south of the Baltic is enough to show that these trade relations were not insignificant. But compared with what was to be gained in Italy, the harvest in the East was at that time still scanty. . . . A connection with the Mediterranean and therefore with world trade could be won by peaceful means in Italy, but it was doubtless a temptation to take one of the richest countries of Europe by conquest. The booty from Slavic lands can by no means be compared to the taxes, tributes, custom duties, and income of all kinds which were available in Italy. Added to the economic wealth was the treasure in art works and relics, an advantage not to be underestimated in the tenth century and one which the Slavs could not compete with. Countless stones, columns, and relics were taken north and used in the construction of churches during the Ottonian period.

Above all, however, it should be observed that considerably greater profit could be earned in the south with considerably less risk than was necessary in eastern operations. It has recently been correctly asserted that making war between the Elbe and the Oder was extraordinarily difficult, even though it does not necessarily follow from this that it was much easier in Italy. To be sure, the roads and victualling opportunities were appreciably better than in the impassible and desolate lands of the Slavs. But the march over the Alps was not easy, and in summer the stopover in most Italian landscapes was probably not much more pleasant than a winter stay among the Slavs. Above all, however, purely military uprisings were scarcely easier to put down in Italy than in the lands to the east. The Slavic strongholds could hardly have been more difficult to besiege and conquer than the cities and fortresses of the Italians. The military history of the period shows that the German armies got the better of towns and cities only with great difficulty; Otto the Great essentially failed in the art of the siege in the cities of France as well as with those of South Italy. Yet however that may be, the decisive question seems to be not whether warfare was simpler in the South than in the East, but the fact that in the South—at least in Lombardy—it was generally not necessary to wage war at all. . . . in 951 the magnates in Berengar's empire went over to Otto for the most part, and he was able to enter Pavia without a battle. In 961 he was called to that country by a strong party; then too Berengar's crown fell to him almost without clash of swords, and later the opposition to German rule was quite limited. Obviously the German regime was more convenient and popular than that of a local king. Among the Slavs there were renegades and groups than leaned to the Germans, but usually their intrusion was greeted by stubborn bitter opposition. The conquest of the Slavic lands required much greater exertion than did that of Lombardy. Can anyone be surprised that the German king did not renounce the richer annexations of the South for the poorer ones of the East?

Nevertheless, in all this there is one thing to ponder. What we have just said in support of Otto's Italian policy can be applied to his intervention in North Italy. The long absence of the king from Germany and the waste of political and military energies, which were thus drawn away from internal and eastern policy, were nevertheless determined less by the annexation of the Lombard empire than by Otto's advance to Middle and Southern Italy. If he had been satisfied with the North, the second expedition to Italy, which was prolonged by the thrice-repeated trip to Rome, would probably have claimed considerably less time and strength, and the third expedition to Italy—the longest of all—might well not have been necessary.

This brings us to a question which, as far as I know, has up to now hardly played a part in the discussion of Otto's Italian policy. That is the question . . . of whether Otto's imperial policy is to be evaluated as a single phenomenon, or whether it would not be more correct to judge the different phases of this policy individually and therefore under the particular circumstances. That is, if the conquest of North Italy is judged expedient and appropriate from the standpoint of the politics of the tenth century, must the intervention in Rome and against the Greeks be similarly viewed?

We have already established above that the possession of North Italy was already assured for the German king even without the possession of Rome and without the war against the Byzantines. Now it is completely indisputable that it must have been extraordinarily tempting for Otto (and thus psychologically understandable) that after he went to Pavia he should go on to Rome. It is understandable (if not to the same degree) that after he had received the imperial crown in Rome, he should measure himself in South Italy against the king of the Greeks. But what is psychologically understandable is not always necessarily what is politically correct. The conquest of North Italy cannot be "justified" by the necessities of the Ottonian state, but solely from the fact that it offered itself as an easy and fruitful prize to the German king. Was the situation in Rome the same?

The conquest of the Eternal City can be justified on the ground of German necessities as unconvincingly as can that of Pavia. To be sure it also meant a gain of power. But didn't a considerable lust for power match this prize of power? Sovereignty in Rome was not as far-reaching and profitable as in the North, and it was much less certain. Whereas the maintenance of the Lombard empire caused hardly any trouble, Otto had to march against Rome repeatedly, and even so he achieved nothing more than a quite fleeting relationship.

A glance at the following decades and the next century and a half already shows us that the situation remained the same. Sovereignty in Rome was and remained precarious, and it made increasing trouble for the German king, which finally reached its zenith and its catastrophe in the Investiture Struggle. The situation in North Italy, on the contrary, was in essence unassailably secure, and this was proven during the early stages of the Investiture Struggle. I believe in this connection that the Roman policy of some German kings before and after Otto was treated as less important than the North Italian policy—that it was in fact incidental. This is clearly true for Charles III and Conrad II, and to a certain extent also for Arnulf of Carinthia and for Henry II.

It is not always possible to say unequivocally whether a policy is right or wrong. At least it seems better to me in the current state of the discussion to be cautious in judging Otto's Roman policy. On the contrary, I believe his South Italian policy must be viewed as ticklish at best. Though it may seem psychologically understandable, it was still not necessary either for the importance of Germany or for the sovereignty of Pavia or Rome. It was essentially fruitless and cost the Emperor a series of unsuccessful campaigns and four years that might have been profitably turned to account in other areas in his sphere of influence.

The Italian policy was not created for the security of the German state against dangers threatening it, but for the sake of taking the offensive and for conquest, for the spread of power beyond German borders and beyond German national requirements. Whoever has found something of self-defense in the imperial policy will sympathize with it, and whoever thinks about

power and the application of power . . . may be inclined to condemn the policy. I am more skeptical and pessimistic about
Otto's policy in general and especially in its ethical foundations
than are his defenders . . . one must remember in order to be
fair that Otto with his policy of conquest did not stand alone
among the rulers and lords of his time. He only did what the
others did or attempted to do on the borders of their empires
(only with less power and therefore with less success).

Moreover, he was summoned by a strong faction in Lombardy
and then was permanently recognized and supported; in the
same way he was urged by the Pope or a Roman party to inter-
vene in Rome, and the princes of Capua and Benevento went
over to him of their own free will. All this means that his intervention looks like a justified and hoped-for reorganization of
Italian relations rather than a veritable annexation [by Germany.]

To reduce to a simple formula the answer to the question of
the harm or good of great universal historical events . . . reminds one of the laughable attempt to square the circle. Nevertheless, historical thought always revolves around such problems
. . . and so I want to write down once more the banal sentence which is in the introduction even though I will be run-
ning the same risk as before: in Otto's imperial policy neither
the usefulness nor the damage was so great as the contradictory
directions of modern research usually claim; on the whole, however, the Italian policy had more advantages than disadvantages.
If the latter were not the case, it would hardly be understandable that Otto's predecessors Arnulf and Henry I as well as his
successors pursued policies similar to his. Admittedly this policy
was not politically "necessary." Though it cannot be condemned
as harmful for Otto's time, it appears in a different light from
what it must have seemed to those who were convinced of its
"necessity." That is true even for Otto's time; it is also em-
phatically true for later developments . . . [which] we know finally ended with a catastrophe. Whoever comes from the town
hall is always wiser, and it would undoubtedly be senseless to
make Otto the Great responsible for this catastrophe.

Who could have foreseen what would happen a couple of
centuries later under altered circumstances? And why didn't his
successors give up his policy when it became dangerous to a

degree that the tenth century could not yet foresee? This much remains certain: the road that Otto took was seductive and ultimately led to a precipice. Although medicine at first may save the life of a patient, it is also held responsible if harmful consequences result later on. But if the patient didn't need the medicine in the first place, it is deplored as poison. In the middle of the tenth century the German state was healthy without doubt. It had developed on its own since the treaty of Verdun; it had overcome the difficult crises of the turn of the ninth century and had risen to be the strongest power of the West: it did not need to take the road over the Alps in order to exist any longer and to flourish. To be sure, it may be true that this path at first secured a more glorious existence for the German Empire, but if the end is kept in view, the impression of brilliance grows dimmer. . . .

# 9    *Carl Erdmann*

*Carl Erdmann (1898–1945) habilitated at the University of Berlin in 1932 and was appointed to the Epistolae section of the Monumenta Germaniae historica in 1934. But in 1935, his promising academic career was cut short by the Nazis: they refused to allow him a university appointment "because of [his] publicly admitted rejection of National Socialism." Erdmann eventually taught small seminars at the Institut für Archivwissenschaft in Dahlem, and he continued to work on the MGH, but he was never awarded the title of professor. He died in military service in Croatia during World War II. Erdmann's principal publications are Die Entstehung des Kreuzzugsgedankens (1935); Die Briefe Heinrich IV (1937); Studien zur Brieflitteratur Deutschlands im elften Jahrhundert (1938); and a posthumous collection, Forschungen zur politischen Ideenwelt des Frühmittelalters (ed. Friedrich Baethgen, 1951).*

## THE OTTONIAN EMPIRE AS *IMPERIUM ROMANUM*

Some six years after the imperial coronation of Otto I (962), Hroswitha of Gandersheim, the Saxon nun and poet, dedicated her poem "The Deeds of Otto" [*Gesta Oddonis*] to the Emperor Otto I and to his son, the future Otto II. In the following years (but still probably during Otto's lifetime) she composed another poetic work, on the history of Gandersheim. These two poems give us our first evidence for the existence of an Ottonian Roman Empire. It is variously called the *regnum Romanum, imperium Romanum, imperium Caesarianum* and *Octavianum.*

Hroswitha was very much aware of the fact that Otto wore two crowns—that he was both king of the Saxons and Emperor of the Romans. . . . At the imperial coronation he received his second scepter and was consecrated a second time; consequently, he was in control of two realms. In point of fact these were Germany and Italy, but Hroswitha called them the Saxon and the Roman Empire.

. . . At first Hroswitha's concept of the Empire was just as limited as that of Benedict of St. Andrea and Thietmar of Merseburg, which . . . excluded Germany. But Hroswitha did not continue to hold this position; rather she emphasized that Otto's dignity as Roman emperor was greater than that of German king, for the imperial throne was "at the pinnacle." Consequently the imperial dignity absorbed the royal dignity.

. . . For this reason Hroswitha apologized for having given Otto the title of king in her narrative before his coronation in Rome (962), because by the time she was writing, he had received the more exalted title of emperor. . . . Therefore, the forms of address which she employs in the dedication both to Otto I and Otto II allude only to the imperial Roman Empire and not to the Saxon realm. [Otto I is called "ruler of the empire of the Caesars, and Otto II is referred to as "jewel of

SOURCE. "Das ottonische Reich als Imperium Romanum," *Deutsches Archiv für Geschichte des Mittelalters*, VI (1943), pp. 421–426; trans. Boyd H. Hill, Jr. Reprinted by permission of the publisher.

the Roman realm."][1] . . . Hroswitha could conceive of the Roman Empire in the broader sense of the whole empire, and she used a narrower and a wider definition of the *imperium Romanum* side by side. But she went even beyond this and recognized a third, still broader, concept of the Roman Empire.

She knew that Otto's empire had universal preeminence, for he was the most famous and powerful king of his time. And she connected the radiance of his sovereign position in his empire with the sovereignty of Rome, noting the expansion of his sovereignty over the Roman world: "many far-flung nations stand in awe of you, and the Roman world bestows manifold honors upon you." Thus Otto's universal sphere of influence continued the ancient Roman Empire. Indeed, Hroswitha conferred upon Otto the Caesarian and Augustan *imperium* and placed him in the same line of succession with the ancient emperors.

By means of this direct connection with antiquity, Hroswitha completely developed the Roman idea—the concept of the empire rather than the idea of Rome proper. She alludes only once to the Eternal City as the capital of the world, and that one reference is in the past tense. Rome the religious city of the apostles and popes is not mentioned in this context at all. On the other hand, she repeatedly speaks of the Roman *imperium* as if it were contemporaneous. It is no wonder that the idea of the Roman Empire meant more to her than the idea of the city of Rome.

A personality like Hroswitha could hardly have had close ties with Rome, and she had certainly never been there. Even ecclesiastical Rome could scarcely have been very important to her. What she knew of the Romans was derived primarily from antiquity, and was literary in character. When she called Otto the emperor of the "mighty Romans," she surely must have meant the Roman people of antiquity, whom she knew from her reading, not the powerless inhabitants of the Rome of her day. Just as her poetry was to a great extent the product of her

---

[1] Erdmann's implication is that in dropping the title "King of the Saxons," Hroswitha assumes that the title "ruler of the Romans" includes it; or, in territorial terms, the Roman Empire includes Germany.

training and education, so was her idea of the Empire. This
explains why she had formed notions about the Empire which
had only partial validity for the politics of her time.

But this gives us a clue to one of the driving forces in the
development of the Ottonian idea, as is proven from the evidence
offered by Gerbert of Reims, the greatest scholar of the tenth
century. For whereas Hroswitha led a rather unremarkable life
in the quiet of her nunnery, Gerbert, on the contrary, was one
of the most influential men of his time. His great opportunity
came when the youthful emperor Otto III summoned him to
court as a tutor in 997. Gerbert triumphantly asserted in the
dedication of a philosophical work written for the emperor:
"Ours, ours is the Roman *imperium!*" In this passage he named
Italy, Gaul, Germany, and the Scythian empire (that is, the
Slavic lands) as power bases. . . . Thus for Gerbert the Roman
Empire consisted not only of the limited Roman area but the
whole territory of Ottonian sovereignty.[2]

Even in his reply to the imperial summons Gerbert referred
to Otto as Greek by descent, but Roman by *imperium.*[3]

This statement is particularly striking: the concept of Rome
consists in the *imperium,* not in connections with the city of
Rome. Gerbert was at home in the ancient intellectual world as
no one else, and so it is understandable that he thought more
about the ancient Romans than about the contemporary ones and
that his ideas were formed by literature. . . . In his mind Roman
power (*Romana potentia*) was accompanied by Roman wisdom
(*Romana sapientia*)—the imperial realm of philosophy, the pur-
suits of the intellect. For Gerbert the renaissance of antiquity
introduced by Otto III began with the revival of scholarship,
even though this renaissance then spread to other fields.

His verses about Boethius illustrate his point of view; here,
his concept of the Roman world parallels that of Hroswitha:

"While powerful Rome passed judgment in its own sphere,
you Boethius Severinus, father and light of the country, held
the reins of government in the office of consul, and were equal

---

[2] Cf. Plate 12 in which the emperor receives homage from four parts of
the empire—Germania, Alemannia, Francia, and Italia.

[3] See Gerbert's letter, p. 34.

PLATE XII.  Manuscript illumination of Otto II or Otto III receiving
homage from four parts of the Empire (Musée Condé,
Chantilly—Art Reference Bureau).

in intelligence to the Greeks for the brilliance of your scholarship. But the Divine Mind controls the rule of the world: Roman
liberty perished under the sword of the wild Goths. You as
consul and exile gave up your distinguished position by a noble
death. Now the ornament of the Empire, Otto III, who gives
great emphasis to the highest arts, has judged you worthy of his
court and has perpetuated the monuments of your labor forever,
suitably rewarding your noble talents."

These ideas had the greatest impact on the young emperor, and
the program of the renewal of the Roman Empire (*renovatio
imperii Romanorum*), whose first effects are already noticeable
in the year 997, can be traced back principally to Gerbert.

In the eyes of the emperor the Roman revival primarily concerned the *imperium*, not Golden Rome itself, and we note here
that the concept of the Roman Empire was not a simple function
of the limited idea of Rome proper, but had now acquired in
addition a certain independence. Rome as a center of influence
had declined, although its literary tradition had become all the
more lively. In the cultivation of the literary heritage of antiquity
the Romans themselves were far behind, and even the Italians no
longer held the lead. To be sure, Italy still had the tradition of
schools of Latin grammar, but they were comparatively unproductive; the cloisters and foundations of the northern countries had surpassed them in certain respects. People like the
Saxon poet Hroswitha and the French scholar Gerbert were
absent from the Italian scene. So it turned out that the idea of
renewal was brought to Rome from the north.

From this vantage point, Otto III can be viewed as a Roman by
*imperium*. He favored and loved the city of Rome because he
wanted to revive the Roman Empire—not the other way around
—and his ideas about Rome were influenced more strongly by
his literary education and intellectual milieu than by the local
tradition and the monuments of the Eternal City.

## 10                    *Walter Ullmann*

*Walter Ullmann was born in 1910 and attended the universities
of Vienna, Innsbruck, and Munich. From 1935–1938, he was assistant
lecturer at Vienna. During the war he came to England and was
appointed University Lecturer in Medieval History at Cambridge in
1949. During 1964–1965, he was visiting professor at Johns Hopkins.
Since 1966, Ullmann has held the title of Professor of Medieval
Ecclesiastical History at Cambridge. He has published* The Medieval
Idea of Law *(1946);* The Origins of the Great Schism *(1948);*
Medieval Papalism *(1949);* The Growth of Papal Government in the
Middle Ages *(1955);* Principles of Government and Politics in the
Middle Ages *(1961); and* A History of Political Thought in the Mid-
dle Ages *(1965).*

---

### IMPERIAL HEGEMONY

The end of the ninth and the first half of the tenth centuries
demonstrate the truism that the Roman emperor was indeed of
vital importance for the functioning of the papacy. The *raison
d'être* of the Roman emperor was the protection and defence of
the Roman Church, but these decades would also show that the
Roman Church depended for its very existence on its protector.
With the disappearance of the powerful Frankish monarchy,
there disappeared also the special protector of the Roman Church
which rapidly began to degenerate in these decades; the popes
climbed down to depths which must be classed unparalleled.
There is every justification for saying that the Roman Church
was tossed about like chaff in the wind at the time when its
"brachium" [arm] was in abeyance.

Ideological advance under these circumstances can hardly be

SOURCE. Walter Ullman, "Imperial Hegemony," *The Growth of Papal
Government in the Middle Ages,* 2d ed. (London: Methuen, 1962), pp.
229-246. Reprinted by permission of publisher and author.

expected: the popes' personalities; the overpowering domination
of the Roman nobility; the frequent changes in the papal chair
itself; the strong influence exercised by women of a shady past
with no less shady ambitions; the depravity of the papal person-
nel—these indeed are not factors conducive to the development
of ideas.[1] Nevertheless, the idea that Roman emperorship could
only be received from the hands of the Roman pontiff, had not
suffered any eclipse.[2] This idea was as important to the new
dynasty in Germany as to the papacy itself. The early Saxons
bear witness to the enduring attraction and fascination of the
empire conception. The foremost of European Rulers, the first
Otto, after his successful Italian campaign, had to return home
in 951 as a mere king: his request submitted to Pope Agapetus
II [946–955] for the imperial crown was refused. It is an illus-
trative sidelight that before his Italian campaign, Otto I had
already ordered the striking of the characteristic imperial *bulla*—
a somewhat premature governmental action.[3]

The appeal of John XII [955–964] to Otto I ten years later
naturally fell on fertile soil: it was the old appeal of the papacy
for protection and defence, couched in terms reminiscent of
some two hundred years earlier. Otto's help was invoked against
the advancing armies of Berengar and his son Adalbert.[4] Otto
eagerly followed the call: he undertook the second Italian campaign in the function of a protector and defender of the Roman
Church having been thus designated by John XII. Otto went
in the capacity of the "brachium Romanae ecclesiae" [arm of
the Roman Church]. On 31 January 962 at the gates of Rome,
through his legates, Otto took the characteristic oath of protection and defence, particularly as regards the papal territories:
and in the function of a protector (in the Roman-papal sense)
he was crowned by the pope on 2 February 962. Eleven days

---

[1] Liudprand records the degeneracy of the papacy in "A Chronicle of
Otto's Reign," p. 19 ff.

[2] Charles the Great was crowned emperor in Rome in 800.

[3] *Bulla* (Lat. for "bubble") refers to the seal with the owner's name and
image which was attached to official documents. In the case of papal bulls,
the seal has given its name to the document to which it is attached.

[4] Co-kings of Italy, 950–961. See Liudprand, "A Chronicle of Otto's
Reign," p. 19.

later he made the compact with John in which he confirmed the Carolingian donations. In his function as a protector he set out to subject the hostile forces in Italy, on 14 February 962.

It was in the following months that Otto's role as a protector in the papal sense changed into one in the royal sense. In the districts which he conquered and which he had recently confirmed as papal territory he made the inhabitants take an oath to himself instead of, as the pope expected, to the Roman Church. To John XII therefore Otto I appeared no longer as the protector whom he had wished to see, but as the oppressor, in no way different from an Aistulph, Desiderius or Berengar.[5] Thus the pope called upon new protectors, against Otto, namely the Hungarians, the Byzantines—and Berengar. To Otto I the pope appeared as a traitor, no better than any other Roman. The insurrection instigated by John made it imperative for Otto that the root of the trouble should be eradicated: hence Otto's return to Rome in November 963, the summoning of Pope John XII before the synod held at St. Peter's under Otto's chairmanship, and the eventual deposition of the pope by this synod on 6 December 963.

On this occasion the compact issued in February 962 was falsified by the insertion of clauses, of which the most important was that which dealt with the promise by the Romans, given on oath, that they would insist on an oath to be taken by the pope to the imperial legates before his consecration. The significance of this lies less in the actual falsification than in the changes made in another document which then served as the model for the *Ottonianum* which has been preserved until this day.[6] That other document was the so-called *Sacramentum Romanorum* of 824 which, we hold, did not contain an oath to be taken by the pope, but the stipulation that, for the sake of being effectively protected, the pope should notify the emperor of his election, so that the pope's consecration should proceed in the presence of the imperial legates. This notification was changed into an oath

---

[5] Pope Stephen II (752–757) had summoned Pepin III "the Short" to his aid against Aistulf, king of the Lombards. Charles the Great put down Desiderius, Duke of Tuscany and later Lombard king, and restored to the Romans the territory which he had illegally seized.

[6] *Ottonianum*—defined in Schramm's article on DO. III. 389, p. 136.

in December 963 and the falsified *Sacramentum Romanorum* served as the basis of the falsification of the original *Ottonianum*. In other words, what was previously laid down in the interests of the papacy, was now modified in the interests of the empire: the idea of protection in the papal sense, expressed in the no longer extant original *Sacramentum Romanorum*, changed into one in the royal sense and was expressed in the falsified, transmitted *Sacramentum Romanorum*.

Whilst originally, therefore, the papacy notified the emperor so as to be protected, mainly against the unruly Romans, the emperor now appeared as the protector in the royal sense of the Roman Church, and the latter became a protectorate of the empire. The root of the papal notification to the emperor was, ideologically, the conception of the emperor as the "brachium" [arm] of the Roman Church; in documentary form this root could be found in the old *Liber Diurnus* [Journal] regulation according to which papal elections had to be announced to the emperor (or to the exarch at Ravenna) so as to be confirmed: the papacy made use of this *Liber Diurnus* regulation, after the creation of the (Roman) empire in the West, but changed its meaning: the emperor should be notified, not in order to obtain confirmation from him, but protection. This papal notification was therefore the signal given to the emperor to act as the "brachium" of the Roman Church: it was the invocation of the service which was the emperor's *raison d'être*, according to the papal point of view. And it was this (papal) idea of protection which was changed into its royal counterpart: the way in which this was done was by falsifying the document which originally contained a stipulation concerning a mere announcement of the papal election to the emperor: this was transformed into an oath to be taken by the pope to the imperial legates. The emperor, according to the *Ottonianum* in its transmitted form, is the supreme protector in the Teutonic-royal sense.

That change in the role of the protector on the part of Otto could be effected all the more easily as this was precisely the role which he had played towards the imperial churches. The ninth and tenth centuries had not only witnessed the exuberant growth of the proprietary church system, which, from an ideological point of view, is characterized by the application of the Teutonic idea of protection to the individual churches, but also the application of the true monarchic principle to all the important bishoprics. That is to say, the *imperium* as a Christian entity and monarchically ruled, was to be given its appropriate ecclesiastical officers in the shape of suitable bishops and abbots. Hence, fundamentally and as regards royal control, there was no difference between a royal proprietary church and any bishopric or abbacy. Both were essential organs of the imperial government—both kinds of churches were subjected to the monarch, and by the mid-tenth century this distinction had been obliterated. Every important church was now an imperial church. To leave the creation of a bishop to an electing body would have been a serious infringement of a correctly understood monarchic principle. And the *Ottonianum* in its falsified form is a clumsy attempt to adapt the Roman Church to imperial conditions: and there was no safer way of so doing than of basing this document on "previous" documents. This arrangement in the *Ottonianum* is the nearest approach to a full transformation of the Roman see into an imperial see.

The coronation of Otto I in 962 is perhaps the most eloquent testimony of the enduring efficacy of that part of the papal theme by virtue of which only the pope of Rome can confer Roman imperial dignity. And five years later—it was another Christmas Day—Otto had his son crowned emperor at St. Peter's. Although Charlemagne served as the model for all three Ottos, his main theme of an unpolitical and religious Romanism had unobtrusively, but steadily, transformed itself into a fully fledged political Romanism: it was this avowed political Romanism which became a permanent feature of the medieval European landscape. This political Roman empire ideology was so firmly entrenched in men's minds that no other imperial conception could hope to be a serious competitor.

To this Romanism, however, the dispensatory role of the pope was axiomatic and fundamental. Only he is a Roman emperor upon whom the pope had conferred the title and dignity. And yet, neither title nor dignity added anything of tangible value to the power of the first Otto. Before his imperial coronation he had been hailed as "caput totius mundi" [head of the whole world] as "dominus pene totius Europae" [lord of almost all

Europe]; his power before coronation was said to stretch into Asia and Africa; he occasionally called himself in several Diplomata before his coronation "imperator augustus"; he was the most powerful European Ruler who could count not only Denmark and Burgundy as virtual satellites, but who also was invoked as an arbiter in France, who interfered in Spain on behalf of the Christians, whose influence was effectively felt in Norway and Sweden, who had strong ties to Anglo-Saxon England—but in spite of all this, he was a mere "Rex." What he did not have was power over Italy. But in order to be a Roman emperor, he had to have control of the geographical Romans. In order therefore to be a Roman emperor he had to exercise some control over the "Romans" who, so to speak, physically epitomized the Romans (= Latin Christians) everywhere. Hence Otto's eagerness to deal with Italian affairs and his emergence as king of Italy—"rex Francorum *et Italicorum*"— on 23 September 951 at Pavia. The king of Italy was the king of the geographical "Romans" epitomized—the later "Rex Romanorum"—and this status was an indispensable preliminary to the dignity of the emperor of the Romans.

The other reason for the Italian campaign of Otto stands in closest proximity to the advance of the Byzantine troops in Southern Italy: they were the armies of him who had never given up the claim to be the true "imperator Romanorum." The Eastern emperor, in Western conceptions, was a mere Greek emperor, and the Ottonian acknowledgment of the Donation of Constantine was the implicit confirmation of the papal point of view that the Roman empire was at the disposal of the pope, by virtue of Constantine's action.

And, so it was held, this Roman empire could never perish: that empire which is, according to tenth-century conceptions, the idolized political manifestation of Christianity, must be defended against him who arrogates to himself the title "emperor of the Romans." This, so it was held, was the proper interpretation of the prophecy of Daniel: the four empires of this prophecy were the Assyrian-Babylonian, the Persian, the Greek and the Roman empires. This fourth kingdom "shall be diverse from all kingdoms and shall devour the whole earth and shall tread it down and break it to pieces." Already widely current in the middle of the ninth century, this eschatological intepretation of the biblical prophecy furnished a strong ideological ferment in the tenth century as also in later times. In a way, this eschatology was a spiritualized teleology of history.

At this stage of the development it is perhaps advisable to state the one point on which both imperial and papal conceptions were in agreement, namely on the exclusive and universal character of Roman emperorship. Because he was the Roman emperor, the medieval emperor surpassed all other Rulers in dignity and excellence.

But as regards the substance of this Roman emperorship the two points of view differed fundamentally. According to the papal standpoint, this dignity is universal, because it is conferred by the Roman Church. The universality of the Church is reflected in the ideational universality of Roman emperorship. The emperor's universality is a reflexion, not indeed in degree, but in kind of that universality which is epitomized in the Roman Church which confers the dignity of emperorship through the medium of the pope. This may be a subtle, though we hold, a necessary distinction. And the emperor is created for the specific purpose of protecting the Roman Church— hence the protector of the Roman Church, itself the epitome of the universal Church, must needs be conceived on the plane of an ideational universality.

On the other hand, the imperial standpoint did not view the substance of Roman emperorship from this functionalist angle. Accordingly, emperorship is universal, because it is Roman emperorship. The Ottonians (and later imperial generations) put upon Charlemagne's empire the complexion of the Roman empire; they interpreted his Romanism in the historical-political sense. To them Charlemagne appeared as the model monarch, *because* he was held to have been a Roman emperor. This imperial view of Roman emperorship was based, in the last resort, upon the ancient Teutonic idea of royal monarchy. Being the strongest monarchs in Europe, the German kings deemed it their right to be the Roman emperors. The conferment of the Roman imperial crown by the pope was a necessary formality of a declaratory character. The substance of this emperorship was monarchic and autonomous, according to the imperial stand-

PLATE XIII. Ivory panal from Milan with Christ in Majesty attended by Otto II, Theophano, and the future Otto III (Castello Sforzesco, Milan—Art Reference Bureau).

point. There is no need for us to comment upon the ideological metamorphosis which Charlemagne had undergone, nor upon the inconsistencies of this point of view which tacitly brushed aside the genesis of medieval Roman emperorship. Genetically and ideologically he had grown out of the patrician of the Romans, and was always considered by his creator an *ad-vocatus*, an *adjutor* [helper], a *brachium* of the Roman Church.[7]

As we have said before, the identification of the *imperium christianum* with the *imperium Romanum* was one of the bequests of Charlemagne. This identification was of considerable weight with later imperial generations, and the temptation to identify both "empires" had by no means spent all its impetus by the time of the [Hohenstaufens]. But, however much, in a rough sense, Charles's identification corresponded to reality, from the mid-tenth century onwards these two terms began to express different ideas: this was one more feature which the imperial point of view disregarded. According to it, the *imperium christianum* was still the same as the *imperium Romanum*. This identification appears as a salient feature of the century between the first Otto's coronation and the third Henry's death [1056]. Hand in hand with this goes—again quite in accordance with the historical-political conception of Romanism—the quickening insistence on the Roman features of the empire, reaching its apogee in Otto III; and with this goes, again for evident reasons, the rivalry with the Eastern emperor and the concomitant borrowing of Byzantine imperial features, and finally the utilization of the proprietary church system for governing the "imperium." These appear to be the salient features of that century. We can but briefly touch on these features and we do this merely in an attempt to bring the contrast between this sytem and its successor into clearer relief.

The title of Otto I for some years after his coronation was the simple "imperator" or "imperator augustus" without the epithet

---

[7] The title "Patrician of the Romans" was awarded to Pepin and his sons Charles and Carloman. Unlike the plain title "Patrician," which was awarded by the Byzantines as a mere courtesy to the Exarch of Ravenna and the Duke of Rome, he who was "Patrician of the Romans" was the protector of the Church. Charles the Great interpreted the title to mean that he should actually exercise control over Church affairs.

"Romanorum." This may or may not have deeper significance, although the assumption cannot be dismissed out of hand that this title without "Romanorum" was considered sufficient indication of the Roman character of this empire. But that this self-same (Roman) empire was also the Christian empire *par excellence*, cannot be legitimately doubted, considering the actual policy of Otto: he appeared as, and was, the foremost protector of Christianity in contemporary Europe. To all intents and purposes Otto considered his empire identical with the Christian empire, that entity which is made up of the Latin Christians.

The intelligentsia of the Ottonian period bears witness to this Carolingian bequest of the identification of the empire with the Christian empire. At first Otto's empire was the "imperium Romanum" pure and simple, so, for instance, in the poems of the nun, Hrotsvita of Gandersheim. To her the empire could bear no other complexion than a Roman one: it was the "imperium Romanum" or "Caesarianum" or "Octavianum." Almost simultaneously another school of thought appears which programmatically identifies the Roman empire with the Christian empire. Its chief representative was Adso of Montier-en-Der.[8] On the basis of his eschatological interpretation of the prophecy of Daniel he entirely identifies the Roman and Christian empires: "Roman" and "Christian" were interchangeable terms and ideas to him. This empire was the last of the four and its idea is therefore imperishable although its material form was nearly ruined. Hence under the presupposition that both empires were ideologically identical, the collapse of the Roman empire would mean the ruin of the Christian empire: the germs of the "Renovatio Romani imperii," the task of the Latin Christian, were contained in this point of view. But when we now look at Odilo of Cluny, a representative of yet another school, though still French, writing in the first decade of the eleventh century, we shall see that, although to him too the idea of the "imperium Romanum" is of crucial importance, it is no longer identifiable with the "imperium christianum." This is all the more important

[8] Adso wrote a treatise about the Antichrist between 949 and 954, which he dedicated to Otto's sister Gerberga, wife of the French King Louis IV (936-954).

since Odilo of Cluny is one of the foremost Cluniacs: with them certainly the idea of a Christian empire begins visibly to detach itself from the idea of the Roman empire. As regards the functions of the Roman empire, there seems no divergence between Odilo and Adso: to both the Roman empire is indispensable for Christianity at large; to both the Christian empire needs the Roman empire as its protector.

Seen against the political and ideological background of his time, the "Wonder of the World," Otto III, may become accessible to understanding. His motto was Charlemagne: his seal was Charlemagne's, upon which was engraved the head of an old man so as to leave no possible room for doubt; and ROMA on the other side of his seal was surrounded by the inscription: RENOVATIO IMPERII ROMANORUM. But the fundamental difference between him and his great model is too obvious to need any comment: for Charlemagne the *Renovatio* was exclusively political and orientated by Christian Rome; for Otto III it was exclusively political and orientated by ancient Rome. Otto's idea behind his *Renovatio* was that of Adso: in order to save Christianity, the fourth empire must be resurrected: the empire of the Romans is the vehicle, the only vehicle, which can raise Latin Christendom from the quagmire into which it had sunk. Undertaken in the interests of Christendom, this "renovation" was to be carried out by the wholesale adoption of old Roman official titles no less than by the wholesale borrowing of Byzantine models. Naturally, as "imperator Romanorum" Otto III could not tolerate that even in a detail the self-styled "Imperator Romanorum" in the East could surpass him. Even the lance as an imperial standard carried before Otto III is reminiscent of the Byzantine model of the emperor's standard. The former purely religious "renovatio" had now turned into a thoroughly political "renovatio": the former's unpolitical Romanism was replaced by a political Romanism.

This "renovatio" however was only a transitory step in the ideological development of Otto III. For after the Gnesen campaign when he adopted the title "servus Jesu Christi," he advanced in 1001 to the height of "servus apostolorum."[9] There is

---

[9] Otto calls himself "servant of the Apostles" in DO. III. 389, p. 65.

in fact a consistent line of development on the part of the young emperor within the space of three years. First he introduces the "Renovatio" in April 998 on his seal; then, on 17 January 1000, he adds to the title "imperator Romanorum" the designation "servus Jesu Christi", this is replaced in the following year by the designation "sacrarum ecclesiarum fidelissimus et devotissimus dilatator" [most faithful and devoted propagator of holy churches]; and lastly there emerges in his title the "servus apostolorum":

> "Otto servus apostolorum et secundum voluntatem Dei salvatoris Romanorum imperator augustus."[10]

The "imperium christianum" is identified with the "imperium Romanum" and hence its leadership must be in the hands of the one "imperator Romanorum." The identity of the two empires entailed that there must be identity of rulership; as head of the Roman empire Otto III was "imperator Romanorum"; as head of the Christian empire he was "servus apostolorum." The government of this one body was concentrated in the one who, by his title, expressed his most intimate relationship with the apostles, especially with St. Peter. Otto III was emperor and "pope." Or in the more familiar terminology of bygone days, Otto III was *rex* and *sacerdos*.[11] The Renovatio of the Roman empire entailed the Renovatio of the Christian empire.

This new double function of the emperor appears first in the famous Diploma which is of particular concern to us [DO. III, 389]. Issued between 18 and 23 January 1001 this document also expresses the double function of Rome itself: Rome is no longer the apostolic city, but the *urbs regia*, hence the capital of the world, and *therefore* the Church of Rome is the mother church of all other churches. It is as a consequence of his double func-

---

[10] "Otto servant of the Apostles and, according to the will of God the Savior, Emperor Augustus of the Romans," DO. III. 389.

[11] As early as November 998, Otto III presided together with Gregory V in a synod at St. Peter's, Rome, in which a Spanish bishop was deposed and another put in his place. This is, we think, a clear instance in which the emperor acting on his claim as an ideational universal *Rex-Sacerdos* intervened in a purely ecclesiastical and organizational matter [Ullmann's note].

tion, the imperial and apostolic, that Otto III has the authority to testify to this:

> Romam caput mundi profitemur, Romanam ecclesiam matrem omnium ecclesiarum testamur.[12]

And because he testifies to this position of Rome, he finds it particularly exasperating that the pontiffs have so much blackened the record of the city.

> (Testamur), sed incuria et inscientia pontificum longe suae claritatis titulos obfuscasse.[13]

Not only have they claimed what is not theirs, but what they had, had sold, spoilt or embezzled. And when all had gone, they came to the emperor asking for more. Asking for more, he exclaims, basing their claims on those false tales which they fabricated under the name of the Great Constantine and which they made the deacon John write in golden letters. The popes base their claims on those other figments by which they say that a certain Charles (II) had given to St Peter "our public goods." "To which we reply that Charles could not give anything away by right. He had given away what he did not possess. Brushing aside these imaginary scraps of paper and fairy tales, *we*, out of our munificence, make a present to St Peter from those territories which are ours. Just as *we* have elected for the love of St Peter the Lord Silvester, our teacher, as *we* have by God's will ordered and *created him pope*, so do we now confer on St Peter through Silvester gifts from our public imperial property." This gift consisted of the eight counties of the Pentapolis. The pope was not, however, the owner of these eight counties, but merely their administrator.

It is plain that according to Otto III the papacy had no right to the territories hitherto claimed as their own. The title-deed of their claim is declared null and void—the Donation of Constantine is a fabrication from which no rights can flow. This fictitious basis of papal possessions must be supplanted by an

---

[12] "We assert that Rome is the head of the world, we testify that the Roman Church is the mother of all churches."

[13] ". . . but the incompetence and stupidity of the popes have for a long time obscured the titles of her fame."

act of the emperor himself. On account of his imperial and apostolic capacity he could not allow any other title-deed to possessions than his own. The Ottonian Donation is therefore the effluence of imperial omnipotence. It is moreover a Donation which is prompted by the recognition of the services which he had received from his former master, Gerbert, now created pope by the imperial will.[14] Perhaps no particular significance should be attached to the omission of the usual designation of the pope as "spiritualis pater noster" [our spiritual father]: but there can be little doubt about the functions allotted to Silvester by Otto: he was no more than the chief metropolitan within the ambit of the "orbis Romanus" [the Roman world].

On the other hand, the Ottonian Donation is also directed against the Eastern aspirations. Not only is Rome—and not Constantinople—the *urbs regia*, but also the Byzantine Church stands in a filial relationship to the Roman Church. Indeed, it is the whole "orbis Romanus" that is seen by Otto in his twofold capacity. According to him, the "orbis Romanus" was nothing else than the political conception of Christianity. Hence, *Roma caput mundi*, and the unity of this universal body politic presupposes unity in its government: Otto appears as the supreme monarch.

But this Ottonian Donation signifies more than the mere assertion of the emperor's imperial and apostolic capacity. It brings into clearest possible relief Otto's function as the supreme monarch and protector. We think that here is the link with the prevalent institution of the proprietary church system, whose ideological strength lay in the king's affording protection to a weak and defenceless body, the sacerdotal hierarchy. In the exercise of his monarchical rule, the king had the right to install the bishop in his ecclesiastical functions: the bishop thereby came under the special protection of his "creator." It is this idea of

---

[14] It seems fairly certain that the choice of the name Silvester by Gerbert aroused some suspicions in his "creator," especially as Otto was familar with the secrets contained in the bosom of the Roman Church which were revealed to his grandfather by John the deacon [Ullmann's note]. The reason that the name adopted by Gerbert worried Otto was that Pope Sylvester I (314–335) was the one who supposedly received the Donation of Constantine.

protection (in the royal sense) which cemented the proprietary church system ideologically. The protection afforded by the "owner" of every bishopric—was the inner ferment of the system, fortified as this was by the oath of fealty taken by the bishop. The bond thus created was a very personal one. As a protector the king had a very natural interest in the maintenance of his property. He could, if he considered it expedient, concede to certain collegiate bodies, the right to elect their superior, but in the case of the important episcopal sees and as the one most directly interested in the administration and organization of his churches, he himself exercised the right to see that a suitable incumbent was appointed: in these cases the king proceeded by simple nomination; and of Silvester II Otto says: "elegimus . . . ordinavimus et creavimus" ["we have elected . . . ordained, and created"].

There is therefore a noteworthy parallel between the protective function of the Teutonic king and the protective function of the prototype of every *Rex-Sacerdos*, Justinian [527–565]. Although in their origins independent, the two conceptions of rulership had so many elements in common that for all practical purposes they were identical. Teutonic and Byzantine ideas in this respect were so similar to each other that the wholesale borrowing of Byzantine ideas and forms by essentially Teutonic rules may have a simple explanation. Both governmental systems relied heavily on the *sacerdotium*, and the Teutonic manner of harnessing the *sacerdotium* to the governmental machinery by way of the proprietary church system was, in our opinion, merely a practical modification of the same principle, perhaps furthered by the prevalent feudal conceptions. To both systems, the Eastern and the Western, it was essential that a *suitable* candidate was appointed for the see. Here we find the principle of idoneity or suitability which was of such crucial importance to the hierocratic system too. But whereas in the latter system the suitability concerned the Ruler himself, in the former it concerned the ecclesiastics, above all, the bishops, and of course the pope. To all three systems, the *sacerdotium* was an indispensable vehicle by which the respective policies were to be carried out. And in a way one might say that the later Investiture Contest was essentially a fight over the control of the *sacerdotium*.

What seems important was that the idea of royal protection was carried by Otto III to its logical conclusion. Indeed, the *Ottonianum* made an attempt at this when it initiated the somewhat clumsy machinery of an oath to be enforced by the Romans from the pope. The *Ottonianum* was a patched-up document which did not make any fundamental pronouncement, and because of this shortcoming the third Otto may have refused to confirm it; he also recognized that the donations contained in the document were based upon slender foundations. But in the Ottonian Donation we have in fact a programmatic declaration of him who was supreme monarch and therefore supreme protector of every one in his "orbis Romanus," including the papacy. And the angry outburst of Otto about the squandering of papal possessions by the pontiffs is the outburst of one who believes that his own property has been the subject of wanton spoliation. Hence a clean sweep has to be made. And he programmatically declares that the pope—in no way different from any other bishop—owes his position to him: he also declares that the pope *qua* pope has no right to territories. The donation to St Peter through the hands of the pope who is to be the trustee of the territories, is the effluence of Otto's imperial and apostolic omnipotence.

Monarchy means supreme rulership carried out by means of the law and the appropriate agencies. For the Ottonian system this entailed a function of the pope which was not unlike that accorded to him by Otto's great model, Charlemagne. Whether or not Otto acknowledged the magisterial primacy of the Roman Church is of no concern to us, but what is of concern is that the jurisdictional primacy of the Roman Church was denied. The pope was not, and could not be, given the right to surround his pronouncements with the halo of a legal sanction. The conception of true monarchy militated against this. The pope is, in Otto's conceptions, the chief priest in the "orbis Romanus," appointed by the "servus apostolorum." The former Justinianean prescription of an imperial confirmation of the elected pope had now degenerated into a straight imperial appointment. This manner of making a pope was, naturally enough, based upon the principle of suitability, and Otto had every reason for finding Gerbert suitable. The spirituality of the papal—as indeed of every sacerdotal—office made it imperative that in this Christian "orbis Romanus" only the best and most suitable should be raised to this dignity. It is at this point that the "reforming" Cluniacs come into the picture, and Otto III himself was very much influenced by Odilo of Cluny. As the supreme protector Otto III, not unlike Justinian, had to see that his empire, Roman and Christian as it was, was given the best men. This astonishing parallelism between East and West led to a still more intensified copying of Eastern features and the adoption of ancient Roman elements, particularly by contemporary littérateurs of which none is perhaps more significant than the *Graphia* circle.[15] And the renascence of Roman legal studies was an inescapable consequence.

To sum up, Otto III's standpoint was focused upon the implementation of the monarchic principle. The monarch rules over that body politic which, by virtue of its universal character, is Roman and Christian. The basis of this view is the idea that this political entity is entrusted to him by God: he as the divinely appointed monarch must therefore rule, that is, guide and direct that body politic, of which the cementing idea was that of the Christian faith. In this sense his empire was indeed Roman—in the other, political, sense the empire could call itself Roman only as a result of accepting papal ideology, according to which the Roman empire was dispensed by the pope. In either sense the ideological weakness of Otto's position is apparent. It was a governmental theory which bore all the germs of its own destruction within itself. Was he functionally qualified to lead a body politic whose substratum was a spiritual element, the Christian faith? Was not his own Romanism the tacit acceptance of the papal theme?

---

[15] The anonymous author of the "Graphia aureae urbis Romae" describes the imperial court about 1030. See Percy Schramm, *Kaiser, Rom, und Renovatio*, 3rd ed. (Darmstadt: Wissenschaftliche Buchgesellschaft, 1962), pp. 193–217.

## 11          *Ernst H. Kantorowicz*

*Ernst H. Kantorowicz was born in Posen, Germany, in 1895. He died in the United States in 1963. Educated at Berlin, Munich, and Heidelberg, he was appointed professor at Frankfort in 1932. In 1934 he went to Oxford as a visiting professor, and to Berkeley in 1939. In 1951, he was appointed professor of history at the Institute for Advanced Study, Princeton. Some of his books are* Kaiser Friedrich der Zweite, 2 vols. *(1927–1931);* Laudes regiae: A Study in Liturgical Acclamations and Mediaeval Ruler Worship *(1946); and* The King's Two Bodies: A Study in Mediaeval Political Theology *(1957), for which he was awarded the Haskins Medal by the Mediaeval Academy of America.*

---

### CHRIST-CENTERED KINGSHIP:
### THE FRONTPIECE OF THE AACHEN GOSPELS

A Romanesque type of crucifix, known as the *Volto santo* [Holy Face] and showing the Crucified with an imperial diadem on his head and the purple around his shoulders, renders perhaps the briefest iconographic formula of at once the regal and the sacrificial characters of the God-man. The compact brevity and terseness of that formula is so striking that the image cannot fail to impress directly: the *Volto santo* is signally *una persona, duae naturae* [one person, two natures]. The theme of the two natures of Christ, of course has often formed the subject of artistic representations, though normally each nature would be figured individually: the newly-born or the cross-bearing Jesus in the

SOURCE. From Ernst H. Kantorowicz, *The King's Two Bodies: A Study In Medieval Political Theology* (Princeton: Princeton University Press, 1957), pp. 61-78. Reprinted by permission of Princeton University Press, illustrated in Plate 14. Cf. Plate 13 (p. 109) in which Otto II and his family are subordinated to the figure of Christ.

PLATE XIV.  Manuscript illumination of Otto II *Christomimetes* (Cathedral Treasury, Aachen—Art Reference Bureau).

lower part of the panel, and in a superimposed register, the King of Glory. In the *Volto santo,* however, the duality is so stirring, and it is expressed so powerfully, that the effect is much stronger here than in the images displaying the two natures separately.

Only in the full flush of the uncompromisingly christocentric period of Western civilization—roughly, the monastic period from 900 to A.D. 1100—could it happen that also the two natures of the imperial christomimētēs [imitator of Christ] ruling on earth were depicted in a similarly brief, if iconographically very different, fashion. The famous miniature in the Gospel Book of Aachen, executed about A.D. 973 in the Abbey of Reichenau, shows the Emperor Otto II enthroned. He is seated on a throne-bench decked, as usual, with a roll-shaped cushion, while his feet rest on a footstool. It is certainly a representative imperial image of state, conventional in the West since Carolingian times; but there is much disregard of artistic custom and convention in the Aachen Codex. The throne is not standing on firm ground as normally it would in the state images of the precious Carolingian and Ottonian manuscripts. It is seemingly poised in mid–air, for the throne as well as the emperor's whole figure are surrounded by a mandorla [almond-shaped design]. Yet the throne stands on earth; it is carried by a crouching *Tellus,* Earth herself, whose hands support the feet of the footstool. At the same time, the Hand of God is reaching down from above, from heaven, either to impose or to touch and bless the diadem on the emperor's head. The divine aureola [halo] framing the Hand of God intersects with the imperial aureola, thus allowing the emperor's head to be placed in the spandrel which is formed by the intersecting haloes.

The image shows three superimposed planes. The upper part of the emperor's figure is surrounded by the four beasts of the Apocalypse, symbols of the four Evangelists, holding a white banderole or drapery. Deep below the emperor's feet, in the foreground of the image, four dignitaries are seen, two archbishops and two warriors, apparently representing the princes spiritual and secular. In the central part, right and left of the footstool, there stand, flagstaffs with purple pennants on their shoulders, two male figures in a gesture of veneration, if not adoration. That they are of very high rank is suggested by their crowns—feudatory dukes or perhaps rulers of the *regna* [king-doms], the plurality of which was needed to indicate the impe-rial dignity. At any rate, they are princes or reguli dependent on the young kosmokrator [ruler of the world] who himself is raised towards heaven or into heaven. We may think of the description of the emperor's power—the power as such—offered, a century later, by the Norman Anonymous. He calls the im-perial potestas [power] grand and holy, the *cooperatrix* [co-operator] of the grace of God and therefore entitled "to treat with the sacraments of the Catholic faith and matters celestial." Then he draws his conclusions:

"Therefore the emperor, by the Lord Jesus Christ, is said to be elevated even unto heaven. Even unto heaven, I say, not unto the corporeal sky which is seen, but unto the incorporeal heaven which is unseen; that is, unto the invisible God. Truly, unto God he has been elevated, since so much so is he conjoined to Him in power that no other power is more nigh unto God or more sublime than that of the emperor; yea, all other power is inferior to his."

These are the very ideas which the miniature displays: the emperor elevated unto heaven (*usque ad celum erectus*), all earthly powers inferior to his, and he himself nearest to God. Most startling, in view of the miniature, is the concept of the *imperator ad celum erectus* [the emperor elevated to heaven], since this is exactly what the artist painted. Could he have known that phrase? Chronologically, there would be no difficulty. The phrase is taken from the so-called *Collectio Hispana* or *Isidoriana,* a collection of canons composed probably in the seventh cen-tury, ascribed to Isidore of Seville, and later fused with the Pseudo-Isidorian collection. That the phrase actually originated in the *Hispana* is obvious for a simple reason: only in that collec-tion do we find a textual corruption of the acts of the Council of Chalcedon [451] at which one of the bishops modestly said that God *imperatorem erexit ad zelum* [i.e., *fidei*] ["aroused the emperor to zeal," that is "to faith"]. In other words, a scribe copying the canons of Chalcedon misread the text and changed *ad zelum* into *ad celum;* and this erroneous reading must have reached, perhaps through the channels of Pseudo-Isidorus, the

Norman Anonymous for whom even that great forgery in favor of the hierarchy could turn into grist brought to his royalist mill. The reading is merely an error, though an error remarkable by itself, since it shows how easily any extravagant exaltation of the imperial power could flow from the pen of a scribe in those centuries.

For the present purpose we may forget about the *Hispana* text, for it is most unlikely that the Reichenau painter knew that corrupt reading when he pictured the *imperator ad celum erectus*. Nevertheless, it remains a fact that the glorification of the emperor as displayed by the miniature of the Aachen Gospels by far surpasses anything that was customary in Eastern or Western art. The image shows the emperor in the *maiestas* [majesty] of Christ, on the throne of Christ, holding his open and empty left hand like Christ, with the mandorla of Christ, and with the animal symbols of the four Gospels which are almost inseparable from the images of Christ in Majesty. An ivory book cover from St. Gall and another one of the early tenth century, now at Darmstadt may bear out this assertion. These parallels demonstrate that the emperor appears not simply as the *vicarius Christi* [vicar of Christ] and human anti-type of the World Ruler above, but almost like the King of Glory himself—truly the christomimētēs, the impersonator and actor of Christ. It is as though the God-man had ceded his celestial throne to the glory of the terrestrial emperor for the purpose of allowing the invisible *Christus* in heaven to become manifest in the *christus* on earth.

Related ideas were carried through iconographically by other means as well. Attention has been called recently to the mosaic in the Martorana at Palermo, representing the coronation of King Roger II [King of Sicily, 1112–1154] at the hands of Christ, where the desired effect of making the God manifest in the king was achieved by a striking facial resemblance between Roger and Christ—a duplication which has its parallel in certain images of the Ottonian period, and has its precursors in imperial coins of the third and early fourth centuries . . . . In the Aachen Gospels, however, the emperor's assimilation with Christ is indicated, not by means of facial and physiological resemblance between ruler and divine prototype, but rather by a christological and indeed meta-physiological resemblance: the image, to say it immediately, represents the emperor's two natures, human and divine, or rather, in the language of that age, a ruler "human by nature and divine by grace."

Any interpretation of the image must proceed from the mysterious white banderole or scarf-like drapery which so obtrusively demands the attention of the spectator. It is carried by the four Evangelists represented by the apocalyptic symbols, and it is carried in such a fashion that the two tips of the banderole barely touch the crowns of the *reguli*. A fold of the band itself seems to divide the emperor's body: head, shoulders, and chest are above the borderline; arms, trunk, and feet remain below. The observation was made long ago that the white drapery separates heaven from earth. In fact, the emperor's head not only touches heaven, but is in heaven, or beyond the heavens. whereas his feet on the footstool are carried by the subservient *Tellus*, a feature of world dominion reminiscent of the Barberini Diptych, of Gandhara and later Buddhist monuments, or, above all, of a contemporary ivory in which *Terra* supports the feet of the crucified Christ . . . .[1] The interpretation of the image actually hinges on the interpretation of the banderole, and the understanding of both the details and the whole will be considerably simplified once we know what the banderole designates.

The white scarf is not a band or a banderole at all, nor is it merely an ornamental drapery: it is a veil. It is actually THE VEIL, that is, the curtain of the tabernacle which, according to the oldest Eastern tradition, symbolizes the sky separating earth from heaven. Speculation about the meaning of the veil was at all times alive in the East, since the curtains of the iconostasis, which have a definite function in the rites of all Eastern

---

[1] See André Grabar, *L'Empereur dans l'art byzantin* (Paris, 1936), 48ff, and pl. iv, for the Barberini Diptych . . . . For Gandhara, see Hugo Buchthal, "The Western Aspects of Gandhara Sculpture," *Proceedings of the British Academy*, XXXI (1945), Fig. 29, a feature repeated over and over again. For the Gotha Crucifix carried by a crouching *Terra*, see [Adolf] Goldschmidt, [*Die Elfenbeinskulpturen aus der Zeit der karolingischen und sächsischen Herrscher* (Berlin, 1914)], II, pl. ix, Fig. 23 [Kantorowicz's note].

Churches, actually demanded some explanation.[2] However, the interpretation of the veil of the tabernacle as "sky" was very common in the West as well. Bede [672–735], for example, in his work *On the Tabernacle*, explains in full agreement with the Eastern expositors that "the veil figures the sky." He adds that when once a year on the Day of Expiation the high priest of Israel passed through the sky-curtain of the tabernacle in order to offer (Leviticus 16: 12ff), he—like Christ, the eternal High-priest—actually "entered into heaven itself" (*in ipsum coelum intravit*). Now the sky-curtain, according to Exodus (26: 31f), was hung before four pillars. Those pillars were often identified with the four corners of the world, but full scope was also given to other interpretations. Bede, for example, identified the four pillars with "the powers of the celestial hosts, adorned with the four virtues," and later interpreters of the tabernacle claimed that the pillars signified Apostles. In the Reichenau miniature it is neither the celestial hosts nor the virtues nor the Apostles that are credited with representing the four pillars holding the veil of the tabernacle, but the four animal *virtutes*, the Evangelists—logically, insofar as the picture precedes a Gospel Book.

It would be pleasant to think that the artist, when introducing the four Gospel animals, intended also to allude to the emperor's missionary task. After all, the emperor was "crowned by God" *ad praedicandum aeterni regis evangelium*, "to preach the Gospel of the Eternal King." This idea was expounded in the official "Mass for the King," it was repeated in many a Coronation Mass, and it was programmatically adhered to by the Ottonians in their missionary policy. The combination of veil and animals, however, derived directly from the Carolingian models which the artist followed. These technicalities, interesting though they are, shall not occupy us here. Nevertheless, it should be mentioned that in several Carolingian Bibles a picture is found showing the four animals with the throning figure of a man who holds a veil over his head. . . . This miniature conveniently supports the interpretation of the banderole as "sky," for the

---

[2] Iconostasis: in the Eastern Orthodox Church, the partition decorated with icons which separates the altar section of the church from the choir or nave.

veil billowing above the head of that male figure descends directly from the veil which the ancient Roman god *Caelus* holds over his head to indicate the sky . . . .

Symbolically the veil of the tabernacle was said to separate heaven from earth. According to its original function, the curtain separated, within the Temple, the sanctuary from the Holy of Holies (Exodus 26: 33). To Bede, who again argues along customary lines, this division of the Temple appeared as a symbol of the Church which itself was twofold: men peregrinating below on earth, and saints as well as angels ruling above in the heights. At this reflection about the twofold Church, Bede arrived because the veil reminded him of the two natures of Christ the Mediator who was, at the same time, on earth the man Jesus and in celestial eternity the co-ruler of God. Bede, at least, offers a clue to help us understand the separating curtain as an indication of the two natures of Christ.

Bede's seemingly strange association will become less cryptic when we turn to another peculiar item of the Aachen miniature: the apparently gigantic stature of the emperor whose feet rest on earth while his head is in heaven. Incidentally, there exists a miniature of Otto's contemporary in the East, Emperor Basil II, who likewise towers like a giant from earth to heaven . . . while his defeated enemies crouch below. The giant figure, of course, was a distinguishing mark not only of Hellenistic and Roman or Byzantine emperors honored by colossal monuments, but also of Christ. It was a feature well known in early Christian popular belief, especially in the gnostic and docetic circles which may even have drawn from a Rabbinic tradition concerning Adam: "The first man extended from the earth to the firmament." However, the vision of a giant Christ was orthodox as well. It was kept alive within the Church through the 18th Psalm: "He hath rejoiced as a giant to run his course." And although in the Psalm the giant stature of God—Justin parallels him with the mythical Heracles—has no obvious relation to the two natures, Saint Ambrose [c. 340–397] nevertheless speaks in that connection of Christ as the *gigas geminae substantiae* [giant of twinned substance]. The Psalm has been taken subsequently as an allusion to either the Incarnation or the Resurrection and Ascension of Christ. And perhaps the Ambrosian

"Giant of two substances" should be linked to a standard interpretation of the head and feet of Christ which was current in the East. "The head means the godhead of Christ; the feet, his manhood," writes Cyril of Jerusalem [c. 315–386]; and it was quite common, especially in connection with "the feet like unto fine brass" of the Revelation (1: 15), to explain that the feet of Christ indicated the Incarnation.

The intellectual climate of the Ottonian period would probably allow us to take Greek writings into consideration. However, we do not need to seek succour from either Gnostic authors or Eastern theologians to explain the Reichenau miniature. *A priori* it would appear unlikely that the master of the Aachen Gospels should have been inspired by other than conventional material for his unconventional image. Decisive, in fact, is a source not at all obscure: Augustine's *Enarrationes in Psalmos* [interpretations of the Psalms], which may serve also to illustrate the Ambrosian *gigas geminae substantiae*. When interpreting Psalm 91, Augustine exclaims: "Oh Christ, who sittest in heaven on the right side of the Father, but art with thy feet and thy limbs struggling on earth." Augustine, on that occasion, repeated only an idea treated by him at greater length in his exposition on the preceding 90th Psalm. Here he discusses the word "tabernacle" (v.10), and points out that the word was used of the human flesh. "The tabernacle of God is the flesh. In the flesh the Word has dwelt, and the flesh was made a tabernacle for God." Augustine then continues: "In this very tabernacle the Emperor [i.e. Christ] has militated for us—*In ipso tabernaculo Imperator militavit pro nobis.*" Once more he remarks on that occasion: "He is far above all heavens, but his feet he has on earth: the head is in heaven, the body on earth." And so as to preclude every possibility of a dichotomy and preserve the dogmatic "One person, two natures," he adds: "But we should not believe that the head is separate from the body: there is a discretion in space, but a conjunction in love."

It should be mentioned that the Augustinian exegesis of that Psalm was repeated many times and was generally known. It passed into the ordinary gloss on the Psalter; it is found in the Psalm Commentary ascribed to Bede; it appears later in the marginal glosses of the Canterbury Psalter and in the Exposition on the Psalter by Peter the Lombard, and can probably be found in many other writings as well.[3]

The Reichenau artist did not come about those passages merely by chance. Commissioned, as apparently he was, to design a triumphal image of the emperor, he naturally turned to Psalm 90 and consulted Augustine's commentary. For Psalm 90 was the great Victory Psalm, the "imperial" Psalm *par excellence* according to oldest tradition, because it contains the famous versicle (v.13): "Thou shalt tread upon the adder and the basilisk, the lion and the dragon shalt thou trample under feet." In fact, this Psalm was for many reasons so irresistibly imperial that the very few and rather exceptional representations of Christ in the full uniform of a Roman emperor—golden armour and imperial shoulder fibula with three pendants. . .—are all connected with Psalm 90: 13, although otherwise "gods in uniform" were a subject not too rarely depicted in late Antiquity. There cannot be the slightest doubt, therefore, but that the Augustinian exegesis of Psalm 90 prompted the artist to represent the living emperor Christ-like as *Imperator in tabernaculo militans* [military emperor in the tabernacle]. As a result, he turned the ambivalent word *tabernaculum* from its figurative meaning ("flesh") back to its original meaning of tabernacle: thence in his picture the "veil of the tabernacle," which became to him also an essential stage property for dividing the emperor's body and indicating the geminate nature—*pedes in terra, caput in coelo* [feet on earth, head in the heavens].

To understand the specific function of the veil, another iconographic pattern has to be considered: the image of the Ascension of Christ showing only the feet of the Incarnate whereas body and head have already disappeared in heaven. Perhaps, though not necessarily, the concept of *Christus Gigas* was influential too.

*Maximus ecce gigans scandit super astra triumphans (Lo, the greatest giant strides over the stars in his triumph)*

---

[3] Peter Lombard (c. 1100–c. 1160) was bishop of Paris and author of the *Sententiae* or sentences, a handbook of theology. Though not a very original work, it gained immense popularity.

reads a verse inscription explaining an Ascension picture in the Gospels from Bamberg of the early eleventh century. At any rate, the new type of Ascension imagery, very common in the thirteenth century and the later Middle Ages, made its first appearance around A.D. 1000 in two Anglo-Saxon manuscripts as well as in the Bernward Gospels from Hildesheim. . . . It marks a complete break in the whole Western tradition as well as with Eastern inconography. Hitherto the Ascension had been depicted in the forms of an antique apotheosis or of an epiphany; now, however, Christ does not become manifest, he disappears in Heaven. That is to say, whereas *caput et corpus Christi* are in heaven, the feet alone—the symbol of the Incarnation—remain as a visible token of the historical fact that the Incarnate has migrated on earth. Moreover, it is the sky that divides the body of Christ and suggests the two natures, just as the "sky" divides, in the Reichenau picture of Otto II, the body of the emperor.

The sky—that is, the veil of the tabernacle—in the emperor's image still demands some comment. The veil is held by the Eagle of John and the Angel of Matthew in such a fashion that the fall of the fold leaves head, breast, and shoulders as well as the brachial joints of the emperor "above," that is, in heaven whereas the body, including the hands, remains "below." We have to remember that head, breast, shoulders, and brachial joints were the places where the emperor was anointed with holy oil. Those parts of his body therefore refer, so to speak, to the *christus domini*, whereas trunk and limbs are those of an ordinary man. One might be surprised to find that the hands are below, not above, the veil, since the hands of kings were anointed too. But this detail happens to be correct: the anointment of the hands was not the custom at the imperial coronation nor was it as yet used at the German coronation of Otto II in Aachen (961), though it was introduced a little later, in an Order of the Coronation dated between A.D. 980 and 1000.

More difficult is the explanation of the remaining parts of the veil. The Lion of Mark and the Ox of Luke dangle the ends of the curtain so skillfully that the tips just touch the crowns of the two *reguli* [princes] who flank the emperor's footstool, that is, his feet which "militate on earth." This feature has been borrowed from the Carolingian models in which we notice that the tips of the veil just touch the mouths of Lion and Ox who, playfully like little dogs, snap at the loose ends. . . . In the Aachen Gospels, however, the touching of the crowns of the *reguli* apparently has a more definite meaning. No better explanation could be found than the words of the Gospel of St. Peter where the author narrates the events at Christ's Resurrection: The soldiers, on guard at the tomb, see two angels descending from above and entering into the sepulchre; then they see "how there come back from the tomb three men [instead of two]; and the two support the One; and of the two, the heads reach *unto* heaven; but the head of the One, whom they support, towers *beyond* the heavens." This would fit almost perfectly the scene as depicted by the Reichenau master. The heads of the two *reguli* "reach unto heaven," that is, unto the tips of the veil representing the sky; but the head of the central figure, the emperor, "towers beyond the heavens."

Unfortunately the painter of the Aachen Gospels could not possibly have studied the apocryphal Gospel of Peter of which no evidence shows us that it was available in the West. But even if we have to rule out the Gospel of Peter as a possible source of inspiration, it may yet help us understand the intentions of the artist. In accordance with Augustine's interpretation of Psalm 90, the artist had to show that the emperor's head was *longe super coelos*. He could, however, demonstrate most conveniently that the head was "far above all heavens" by allowing the sky to touch the crowns of the princes dependent on the emperor: their heads reach *unto* heaven or unto the sky, but the head of the emperor towers *beyond* the heavens. It is a purely artistic expedient which does not seem to demand further textual interpretation; it was supposed to be self-explanatory.

Therewith another detail of the picture falls in its proper place: the four figures below, the princes spiritual and secular. If the uppermost plane represents a sphere "above all heavens," and the middle plane a sphere below heaven but reaching "unto the sky," then the lowest tierce [third] would plainly indicate sub-celestial "earth." In fact, this particular meaning of the tripartition is countenanced by Carolingian manuscripts. The Trier Apocalypse, for example, or the Bible of San Paolo . . . show the *Maiestas Domini* in a similar fashion: in the uppermost

tierce we see Christ with the four animal symbols; in the middle
tierce, there are twenty-four elders, their bodies on the level
of the knees and feet of the Saviour and their haloes touching
the sky; and in the lowest tierce moves the unhaloed crowd
with John or Isaiah respectively in the right corner where in the
Aachen Gospels the clergy has its place.

The Carolingian models are important to us because they are a
commentary where the Reichenau artist follows them, and they
are most revealing where he chooses to deviate. A comparison of
the Aachen miniature with the famous Carolingian throne images
—for example, of Charles the Bald [875–877] in the Vivian
Bible and in the *Codex Aureus*—exhibits that point very
clearly. True, there is a veil also in the Carolingian miniatures;
it is attached to the pillars of the canopy . . . vaulting the throne.
But the veil does not overcut and divide the ruler's body; it
separates his head *from* the Hand of God. In the Reichenau
miniature, however, the emperor's head pushes through the curtain or "sky" so that the *dextera Dei* [right hand of God] is now
in direct contact with the head of Otto; moreover, the sky-line
itself now divides the emperor's body in two sections, one supra-
celestial and the other sub-celestial. The comparison explains
also the function of the four animal symbols as carriers of the
veil: the curtain attached to the pillars of the throne canopy
does not suggest the word "tabernacle" nor could it convey the
meanings of "sky" and "far above all heavens" which the
Reichenau painter obviously wished to express. Moreover, the
very presence of the animals as well as the mandorla surrounding
the emperor indicate that he is in the place of Christ, the Emperor "militating for us in the tabernacle." Finally, the veil
dividing the body emphasizes that the emperor on earth has in
common with Christ the two substances—human by nature,
but divine by grace and by consecration.

All this results from a philosophy of state which is very different from that suggested by the Carolingian throne images. It is
true, the Hand of God the Father emanates the divine blessing
and grace also on the Carolingian monarch, and there is a relationship between the ruler on his throne and the far remote
Father in Heaven; but Christ is absent from those scenes. The
Carolingian concept of a David-like kingship was decisively

theocentric: "Thou art the vicegerent of God, and the bishop is in the second place only, the vicegerent of Christ," as the English scholar Cathwulf wrote to Charlemagne.

Nothing could have been more contrary to the Reichenau painter. His emperor is in the place of Christ, and the hand stretching down from above is surrounded by a cross-halo: it is probably not the hand of the Father, but rather that of the Son. In short, the Ottonian concept of rulership displayed by the Reichenau artist was not theocentric: it was decisively christocentric. A hundred years or more of Christ-centered monastic piety have affected also the image of rulership. In fact, the unique Reichenau miniature is the most powerful pictorial display of what may be called "liturgical kingship"—a kingship centered in the God-man rather than in God the Father. As a result, the Reichenau artist ventured to transfer to the Ottonian emperor also the God-man's "two natures in one person." No less distinctly than the Norman Anonymous in his tractates has the master of the Aachen Gospels expounded the concept of the ruler's *gemina persona*.

## 12                    *Percy Schramm*

*Percy Schramm was born in 1894. He was appointed lecturer at Heidelberg in 1924, and moved to Göttingen as professor in 1929 where (except for the war years) he has been ever since. Other than* Kaiser, Rom und Renovatio, *which appeared in 1929, he has published* Geschichte des englischen Königtums *(translated in 1937 as* History of the English Coronation); Der König von Frankreich *(1939);* Hamburg, Deutschland und die Welt *(1952—Hamburg was Schramm's birthplace);* Herrschaftszeichen und Staatssymbolik, *3 vols. (1954–1956);* Sphaira-Globus-Reichsapfel *(1957); and* Kriegstagebuch des OKW IV, *1944–45 (1961). He is a member of the Mediaeval Academy of America, among other organizations.*

SOURCE. "Otto III und die Romische Kirche, Percy Schramm, hach Seiner Schenlaungsurkunde vom Januar 1001," Volume XVII of the *Studien der Bibliothek Warburg,* (London: The Warburg Institute, 1929). Reprinted from *Kaiser Rom, und Renovatio,* (Darmstadt: Wissenschaftliche Buchgesellschaft, 1967), pp. 161-176. Translated by Boyd H. Hill, Jr. Reprinted by permission of publishers and author.

## OTTO III AND THE ROMAN CHURCH ACCORDING
## TO THE DONATION DOCUMENT OF JANUARY, 1001

In January, 1001, the Emperor had Leo of Vercelli [999–1026] draft a deed for Pope Sylvester II [999–1003], which is one of the strangest documents of the Middle Ages and was consequently viewed as a forgery for a long time. Since the transmission of DO. III. 389 [Diplomas of Otto III, no. 389] has been verified and its author established, its authenticity is no longer in dispute. One may now merely raise the question—no longer determinable—of whether the deed left the chancery in the regular way and whether the donation was really carried out.

The deed contains the donation of eight counties in the Pentapolis, that area south of Ravenna which had the most extraordinary significance for the Emperor in securing the main route to Rome, but which was also given special attention by the popes, since it formed the other end of the land-bridge hoped for by Rome which connected the east and west coasts [of Italy].[1] Ravenna and the Pentapolis were confirmed for the popes by charter in the Carolingian pacts and the endeavors of the Curia were further rewarded when Otto I was ready for restitution by renewing the pact. [In 962] he handed over Ravenna and the *terra Ravennatium* without realizing to what extent he had thereby renounced all his rights. The Pope [John XII, 955–964] received the gift "with great joy," for in comparison with the preceding era it signified great success even if only a part of the petrified provisions of the pact were really valid.

The question of the Pentapolis arose immediately upon the coronation trip of Otto III [996]. Perhaps during his march through Rome just as in Rimini he claimed imperial rights. In any case it must have been debated in Rome with the new Pope which of them in fact had actual claim to the Pentapolis. An agreement could not be reached and since Otto wanted to go

[1] During the Exarchate of Ravenna, the Pentapolis Maritima or "Five Maritime Cities" were ruled over by one governor. The five cities were Rimini (ancient Ariminum), Pesaro, Fano, Senigallia, and Ancona.

home, a balance had to be struck which would not encroach upon the rights of either party. These facts are revealed in a letter of Otto to Gregory V [996–999], which Gerbert composed for the emperor on the trip home.[2] It contains the statement that the margraves of Tuscany and Spoleto-Camerino are charged with the protection of the Pope; to him [the Pope] Otto also turned over the eight disputed counties, since he made him his *missus* "for the nonce." [In Gerbert's language *missus* means "legate."] The phrases of the document [DO. III. 389] are carefully chosen in order not to sacrifice any claim and on the other hand not to offend the popes; the goal is expressly stated that by the appointment of the *missus* the obligations owed to the Pope by the people should be secured. How the struggle continued remains in darkness. One can only conclude from the deed of 1001 what were the legal grounds cited by both parties. Furthermore, it can be said that in the interim neither the emperor nor the Pope was moved from his original position, although Otto III had turned his attention to the revival plan of Gerbert, the letter-writer of 996 who had become Pope Sylvester II and who now represented the demands of the Curia.

Two of the legal titles which the Roman Church cited are produced by name in the deed in order to specify why the emperor did not feel bound by them. First of all the Donation of Constantine is mentioned, and it is rejected for the most surprising reason: namely, that it is a makeshift work [i.e., a forgery] falsely attributed to Constantine the Great, from which "John with the mutilated fingers" prepared a copy in gold characters. This fact was ultimately reestablished . . . only in the fifteenth century. How did Otto's chancery come to this conclusion which anticipates the scholarship of centuries?

Here it should be remembered that the John named in D. 389 was a cardinal who was mutilated by Pope John XII and then found asylum with Otto I . . . when the role of the Donation was under investigation in the time of the first Ottos, it was

[2] The letter is dated August 5, 996. See Harriet Lattin, *The Letters of Gerbert* (New York: Columbia University Press, 1961), pp. 271-272.

conjectured that it was this very John through whom the imperial court gained intelligence of the secret workings of the Curia. On the basis of the forgery he supposedly would have been able to prepare only an ornamental copy in the form of a deed. The Curia needed such a copy since it apparently possessed the text of the Donation only in manuscripts like the Pseudo-Isidorian Decretals. After the conjecture mentioned earlier, the Curia also attempted to employ the *Constitutum Constantini* [i.e., the Donation of Constantine] in its dealings with the Saxon emperor, without however having any visible success. In the succeeding era the forgery was known to the court of Otto I, but seems to have been considered a document going back no further than the Carolingian pacts. Liudprand of Cremona alone mentioned it more precisely in the ambassadorial report, for he knew how to play his hand cleverly against the Byzantines [see pp. 29–30].

If Otto III was aware through the tradition of his house that at the time of his grandfather an official of the Curia known to him by name had produced an ornamental duplicate of the Donation, we still cannot say whether he knew anything about the basis of this copy. In the deed it is simply concluded that John himself forged the Donation: the Pseudo-Isidorian basis of his text or whatever is not understood; or if anything was known of it, it was not considered valid. One must indeed be skeptical of information about John from the papal camp, if they were citing the Pseudo-Isidore.

It can thus be readily explained how in the deed of Otto III the conclusion is reached that the Donation of Constantine is a forgery. At what precise time the imperial court was forced to recognize this is not certain. Since Gregory V cited the *Constitutum*, then Otto must already have viewed the deed as not binding at that time, for otherwise he would not have been able to move back the imperial residence to the capital of the Empire which had allegedly been abandoned by Constantine out of veneration for the Apostles.

The diplomatic skill displayed in the deed through by-passing an inconvenient document is even more refined in the rejection of the second of the papal legal titles. After the opening words of the first passage were taken up again, it goes on: "These are also lies whereby they [the popes] say that a certain Charles gave to St. Peter our imperial property. To this we answer that this Charles could not legally have given anything away, since he had already been beaten into retreat by a better Charles, robbed of the imperium, and deposed and overthrown. Thus he gave what he did not possess—in such a manner as he only could give: namely, like one who obtained something illicitly and did not hope to possess it for long." These words are explained only by the "Libellus de imperatoria potestate in urbe Roma" [anon., composed between 877 and 962] . . . whose literal use in D. 389 has been recognized for a long time.

From the context in which these statements are cited from the *Libellus*, it is clear that it concerns the renewal of the pact by Charles the Bald [d. 877], who was driven from Italy by his cousin Carloman [d. 880] (wrongly named Charles in the *Libellus* and the deed). There is only one factual difference between the diploma and its model: according to the *Libellus* Charles the Bald had drawn up the Donation while he was still in power in Rome, whereas according to Otto's deed Charles took this action only when he had already been "driven out, robbed of sovereignty . . . deposed and overthrown." But we can conclude precisely from this difference that the Curia had presented the original pact of Charles the Bald demonstrably originating in France, for it had to contain the citation of the place of issue. However, if the citation of place—"Ponthion" [a palace in eastern France roughly 60 km. south of Reims]— is combined with the citation data of the *Libellus*, then we conclude that Charles the Bald only made the donation at home after his trip to Rome, thus after his rout by the "Better Charles." As a result of this, Charles's pact was without legal basis—the donation of one who was no longer authorized to give anything away.

. . . more important still for the establishment of the legal condition between Pope and emperor than the Donation of Constantine and the pact of Charles the Bald is the *Ottonianum*, the ratification of old pacts which Otto III's grandfather had issued to the Curia in 962. . . . That was the document whose content most interested the Papacy and one which the emperor had to admit was genuine . . . . Otto III did not authenticate the

*Ottonianum* although one might expect that the Curia tried to anchor him anew to this legal basis. This remarkable fact can be gathered from the circumstance that Henry II [1002–1024] renewed the Ottonianum in 1020, without any mention of an intervening document of Otto III. Otto had opposed the *Ottonianum* through his claims to the counties of the Pentapolis in 996 . . . and he conveniently overlooked it again when he bestowed counties on Gerbert as Archbishop of Ravenna which had earlier been donated to the Papacy by his grandfather's deed. Thus Otto acted against the pact throughout his entire reign. How he justified this can be seen in the document in question from the year 1001, for it very prudently does not mention the *Ottonianum* by name, but polemicizes between the lines all the more sharply against it!

. . . why then the surprising invective against the earlier Popes in a deed for the reigning Pope, who was the writer of the letter of 996, the recipient of the counties near Ravenna in 999, the tutor and friend of the emperor; one would not expect him to be the object of a harsh sermon on the misdeeds of his predecessors. This review of the history of papal possessions was necessary, however, in order to win a legal base from which the authority of the *Ottonianum* could be shaken. That was possible only if it were represented as the ratification of an illegal situation which had been secured through false or invalid documents. Wrong could never be right, and when its illegal character was uncovered, the document was likely to be abrogated.

Because of the worthlessness of the privileges underlying the *Ottonianum*, its authority was questioned when the history behind the document was revealed, and this was tactfully managed so that Otto III did not seem to be in open conflict with his grandfather.

One might almost imagine that the deed was composed by Liudprand—so censorious is the judgment of the earlier Popes. But the words of [Arnulf] Bishop of Orleans [971–1003] were uttered in the same tone at the French council of the year 991, and Gerbert himself had noted them down. Leo [of Vercelli] was therefore expressing [in D. 389] the common opinion as well as that of the imperial and ecclesiastical circles and urging that the negligence of the Curia now be replaced by joint secular-ecclesiastical renewal . . . . The Popes, so goes the story, wrongly seized the property of the Church both inside and outside of Rome, dishonored it, and sold it; then they sought to expiate their guilt on the grounds that the Church held the property of the Empire uninjured. Here we see the rebellion over the economic conditions in Italy which Gerbert had come to grips with in Bobbio twenty years earlier [c. 982–984] and which led Otto III to his law of 998. Gerbert as Pope sought new ways to relieve abuses in the economic situation, which also concerned Leo when he drew up the transactions of a synod twenty years later, a synod in which empire and Pope, Henry II [1002–1024] and Benedict VIII [1012–1024], took part. This document . . . shows that Pope Sylvester was not the only one to render harsh judgments on his predecessors. . . .

Document no. 389 contains . . . nothing less than a renunciation of the whole system of imperial donations and authentications by which the political relations between emperor and Pope had been regulated up to that time. All imperial titles which the Popes had fought over in bouts lasting for centuries were discredited; the boundaries of the territory which had been recognized a dozen times for the Roman Church had lost their significance. Even Rome, the abode of the Apostles, was no longer the city of the Pope, but that of the emperor: "in hac nostra urbe regia" [in this our royal city] it says in D. 389. Otto III had so considered Rome since having his residence built in the city. Though the *Libellus de imperatoria potestate* (which Leo used for his deed) claimed that Charles the Great made the Romans into "imperial people," one could say the same for Otto III with equal right. The designation "nostra urbs regia" [our royal city] . . . deliberately says "royal" not "imperial" city because *urbs regia* was an older title of honor for Rome. For centuries it had been the custom to reserve this proud name for Constantinople, but the West appropriated it without hesitation. Originally, however, Rome, and not Constantinople, was the *urbs regia*.

The position accorded to Rome is contained in a short but impressive formula at the very beginning of the deed. It repeats in two ancient metaphors what the deeds and words of Otto illustrate after 998: "Roman caput mundi profitemur, Romanam ecclesiam matrem omnium ecclesiarum esse testamur [we admit that Rome is the head of the World, we testify that the Roman Church is the mother of all churches]. Rome was both the imperial city and at the same time the city of the Apostles, its double nature corresponding to the two sides of the *Renovatio* which had been set in motion.

This formula concedes that if the authorized rights of the Papacy are upheld, the theoretical basis valid up to that time would not be disputed: the doctrine of two powers for the regulation of relations between Papacy and empire remained—the co-existence of *regalis potestas* [royal power] and *sacrata auctoritas pontificum* [sacred authority of the Popes], or of *regnum* [royal power] and *sacerdotium* [priestly power] established by Leo of Vercelli in his Gregorian Rhythm of 998 [a poem dedicated to Pope Gregory V]. But where did Otto wish to draw the line between the two spheres of influence?

However clear the doctrine might be theoretically, the division could be carried out variously in practical life. This question is answered, though not exhaustively, in the second part of D. 389 . . . : "We give to St. Peter what is ours . . . not his own property as if it is ours." Thus the legal basis of this donation seen from the imperial point of view was understandably simple; but what were the changes rung upon this theme? Part I of the imperial deed discussed above is a model of pregnant style, diplomatic skill, and juridical acumen, which cannot easily be paralleled in the whole period of the Saxon emperors. Therefore it is all the more surprising that the remaining part of the diploma, concerned with the intended donation, is so short . . . . The polished formulas used for centuries which compose the text of a normal deed are not only fewer than usual—some are even omitted altogether. And at the end we find a sentence that goes beyond custom which surely demonstrates that the donation was not meant to be limited in time. . . .

If one looks closely at the choice of words in the dispositive section, one finds them amazingly colorless rather than pregnant with judicial insight. We must conclude that it was written that way on purpose: after the traditional formula "ut . . . habeat, teneat et . . . ordinet" [that . . . he may have, hold, and rule] a closing such as "et, quodcumque velit faciat" [and he may do whatever he wishes] has been omitted. Instead of this we find an insertion, which is also found in another deed of Leo. The difference in the phraseology is worth noting:

| *D. 384 (Nov. 1000)* | Leo is permitted for the |
|---|---|
| liceat . . . Leoni . . . ad honorem Dei et S. Eusebii ad nostrum servicium suamque utilitatem omnia . . . habere | honor of God and St. Eusebius [bishop of Vercelli, d. 371] to have everything for our service and for his own utility. |
| *D. 389 (Jan. 1001)* | so that for the honor of God |
| ut ad honorem Dei et S. Petri cum sua et nostra salute habeat, teneat et ad incrementa sui apostolatus nostrique imperii ordinet. | and St. Peter he may have with his own and our welfare, may hold and govern for the growth of his Apostolic See and our empire. |

The gift to the bishopric of Vercelli was made both to accommodate Leo and to strengthen him in the service of the empire; the gift to St. Peter was made for the growth of Sylvester's apostolic office and Otto's empire as well as for the salvation of both their souls.

Every excess in this laconic document is noteworthy. It should be put under a magnifying glass and the questions asked: how can it be an augmentation of the imperium if Otto suddenly gives away eight counties . . .? especially a possession of the greatest importance for the main route to Rome, whose worth must have been clear to Otto since he otherwise would not have retained it in his laws for almost five years. Had he really abandoned the line pursued up to then at the expense of the empire as a sacrifice to his friendship for Sylvester?

This interpretation does not jibe with the fact that the Bull issued at the same time shows adherence to the previous policy, and it is precisely D. 389 that designates Rome, the city of St. Peter, as the city of the emperor. These questions lead into a wilderness of contradictions and improbabilities, from which the only conclusion can be that they are falsely worded and that the way out must be sought in another direction.

It should be added that the brevity and colorlessness of the dispositive portion of D. 389, which is in contrast to Leo's usage elsewhere and above all to the unusually rich content of the "narration," can only be explained on the ground that the consequences stemming from the donation deed were not to be granted without further ado, that it is not a question of a donation in the usual sense, but of a gift whereby the donor does not give away all rights. That this is really the case is proven if one examines who actually received the gift: not the Roman Church, which is not mentioned in the dispositive part of the deed at all, not the Pope and his successors on the papal chair, who are discussed only in the conclusion, nor Sylvester II either, but St. Peter alone! Here the deed makes an altogether precise distinction, which cannot be brushed aside as mere stylistic gamesplaying on the part of Leo, since it is systematically carried through: Otto hands over gifts to St. Peter out of affection for Sylvester, so that the teacher might have something to present to St. Peter in the name of his imperial pupil. As if to prevent misinterpretation, the next sentence repeats once more with similar words that the emperor is presenting and/or giving to St. Peter eight counties which the Pope should "have, hold, and administer." Here, as already mentioned, is left out the statement that he receives power of free disposal; in place of it, however, it is said that the Pope must administer them for the augmentation of his apostolic office and of the empire. The third sentence enumerates the eight counties which the Pope will have *ad ordinandum*, that is, to regulate—all other expressions lacking. To this decree is appended a sentence from the Final Clauses, which only partially fills in the gaps arising from the omission of all stipulations as to undisturbed possession. The Final Clauses, very much altered, speak again of the property which St. Peter has and which he is to get back in case of theft. The corroboration [a subdivision of the Final Clauses] finally closes with the codicil that the donation should be valid for Sylvester and his followers, but this says nothing about the right of property itself.

The peculiarity of these stipulations can only be appreciated if compared to ordinary usage, for example, the way in which Otto's grandfather authenticated the property of the Roman Church. In the *Ottonianum* it says of the recipient: tibi, beate Petre apostole, vicarioque tuo domno Johanni papae et successoribus eius [to you, blessed Apostle Peter, and your vicar the Lord Pope John and his successors] and earlier, in connection with the *Ludovicianum* of 817: aecclesiae tuae beate Petre apostole, et per te vicario tuo . . . domno Johanni . . .eiusque successoribus [to your church, blessed Apostle Peter, and through you to your vicar . . . the Lord John . . . and his successors].[3] So the saint, his church, and its proprietor besides his followers are enumerated one after the other in order to make the donation more secure in every way. The chancery of Otto III here makes use of simpler forms and is contented with naming the Church or its proprietor in the normal way. Of the limited number of deeds in which the saint of the diocese or cloister is mentioned . . . none exhibits the peculiarity of the donation of 1001, for their purpose is always to lock the door from within against any possible challenge and to prevent alienation [of the property]. This is the goal of the *Ottonianum*: the ecclesiastical institution, its proprietor and his successors, as well as the holy property, are named side by side in no particular order—from which we separate the cases which were determined only by the endeavor to alter the expression. These deeds can only serve to authenticate the earlier statement that the medieval saint serves to replace the concept of the "juridical person"; but they do not succeed in explaining the peculiarity of D. 389. It stands out all the more sharply by comparison with Leo's other diplomas, some of which are very close to it in time.

The methods of diplomatics do not lead us any further toward interpreting the donation document, but now the moment

---

[3] The *Ludovicianum* was a document in which Louis the Pious promised to protect Pope Stephen IV (816–817) against enemies including the citizens of Rome. See Walter Ullmann, *The Growth of Papal Government in the Middle Ages*, 2nd ed. (London: Methuen, 1962), pp. 144–145 and 152. See also *Camb. Hist. J.*, XI (1953), pp. 114–128.

has come when we can begin to comprehend it on the basis of the earlier findings. For if in contrast to custom D. 389 distinguishes the rights of the Pope from the more comprehensive rights of St. Peter, it has also been pointed out [above] that Otto III simultaneously reached a special new relationship with St. Peter when the deed was issued with a new title [*Servus Apostolorum*, "servant of the Apostles"]. It follows from this that all rights . . . withheld from the Pope by the donation remained with the emperor, who took cognizance of them for St. Peter in his peculiar position of *Servus Apostolorum*, acting as the legal proprietor of the gift. This separation of imperial and papal competence in the administration of Peter's property must have been very difficult in practice; in any case, it could not have been pinned down from one day to the next, much less carried out. From this point of view, therefore, it is quite understandable that the donation document makes use of vague expressions and leaves out necessary stipulations in order not to prejudice the settlement of these questions. At the same time it becomes clear how the emperor could speak of an augmentation of the empire in spite of the disposal of eight counties, and how he could divest himself of his possessions on the way to Rome, for he by no means gave away the southern Pentapolis, but merely transferred it from the property of the empire to that of a saint whose worldly arm was no one other than himself.

It is immediately clear that the regulation encountered in the Pentapolis cannot be considered limited to this territory. If taken to its logical conclusion, the administration of all of St. Peter's property could have been divided between the Vicarius S. Petri [vicar of St. Peter] and the Servus Apostolorum. It is to be assumed that the emperor's plans actually went in this direction. We know that he resided in Rome and that he designated Peter's city as "his" city; at the same time the Pope had to ask the emperor to defend his rights on the spot, thus in papal territory; and the emperor—not the Pope—functioning only as a mediator directed the conquest of Tivoli [described by Bernward, p. 57] and received the surrender of the insurgents. Circumstances thus forced Otto III to take charge of St. Peter's property. Even the remarkable contradiction that Hungary was raised to a kingdom

"with the leave and at the instigation" of Otto but was simulta-
neously consigned to St. Peter, can be resolved if we assume that
Otto reserved for himself special rights to the property of the
Apostle.[4]

One must be careful not to carry the results derived from D.
389 too far, for the source material is too scanty, and the donation document of 1001 forces one to the conclusion that this
plan had not yet progressed beyond the initial stages. Yet its content can only be clarified from one angle: according to the statements of Adolf Waas . . . the German king was considered the
patron of the Roman Church.[5] He was put in possession of it,
and he therefore had the duty to defend and protect it. This
situation dates from the eighth century and remained in force in
the succeeding period, even though it was the tendency of the
papacy to limit the power of the Carolingians. The patronage
[of the German king] was complicated by the role conceded to
St. Peter in Rome. Adolf Waas designates the king, therefore, as
vice-patron of St. Peter, "who exercises protective custody over
the Roman Church in his name and on his order." . . . this
interpretation of the rights and duties of the king vis-à-vis the
Roman Church also determines his relationship with the Pope,
which was defined in the ninth and tenth century with expressions typical of a patron. "In the treaty of Metz (867) both
parties swore: Mundeburdem autem et defensionem sanctae
Romanae ecclesiae pariter conservabimus in hoc . . . [Moreover,
we will maintain equally the guardianship and defense of the
Holy Roman Church]. Otto I swore at his coronation: cuicum-
que autem regnum Italicum commisero, iurare tibi faciam illum ut
adiutor tui sit ad defendendam terram sancti Petri secundum posse
[Moreover, to whomever I entrust the kingdom of Italy, I will
have him swear to you to be your helper in defending the land
of St. Peter as far as possible], and in his treaty with Pope
John XII are the words: nos in quantum possumus defensores
esse testamur [We testify to what extent we can be defenders].

[4] The coronation of King Stephen took place in either 1000 or 1001 with
a crown which was sent to Hungary by the emperor.

[5] *Vogtei und Bede in der deutschen Kaiserzeit* (*Arbeiten zur deutschen
Rechts- und Verfassungsgeschichte*, Vol. 1), I (Berlin, 1919), p. 144 ff.

Moreover, according to the testimony of Thietmar of Merseburg Henry II swore to Benedict VIII at the coronation [in 1002]: si fidelis vellet Romanae patronus esse et defensor ecclesiae . . . [if he wishes to be a faithful patron and a defender of the Roman Church]." This view of the empire differs greatly, indeed, from that of Otto III, but appears nevertheless to be somewhat akin. If the notion of patronage is carried further, if the attendant claims to the property of St. Peter are converted into tangible rights, if all obligations resulting from donation documents are pushed aside but the duties of protection and defense are taken that much more seriously, then we can comprehend the position of Emperor Otto III in the donation of 1001—except that his relations to Rome, Empire, Peter, and Church were peculiar to him: they were clothed in antique trappings and entailed certain political and intellectual presuppositions. Unfortunately . . . we cannot assert with any degree of confidence that Otto's role as *servus apostolorum* is to be traced back to the basic idea of the emperor as patron to the Roman Church, for if this were the case, then even Otto's renewal plans—surprisingly innovative and essentially shaped for the first time during his life—might ultimately be traced to the traditions of the Ottonian house.

# EPILOGUE

The student who has read the foregoing selections may now go on to investigate the following questions:

Was the Ottonian empire really a renewal of the Roman? How did Otto's involvement in Italy affect Germany?

What was the relationship between the eastern and western empires during the tenth century?

How can we be sure that we are interpreting Ottonian diplomas and charters correctly?

Does the artistic accomplishment under the Ottos compare favorably with that of Charlemagne's day?

What are the roots of the proprietary church system of the eleventh and twelfth centuries?

These are only a few of the questions that might be raised. None has yet been answered to everyone's satisfaction. If you are interested in these problems, you may now start to do research on them.

Research on tenth-century Germany requires a working knowledge of German, since very little has been published on the subject in English during the past generation. A command of Latin is also necessary, for virtually all of the sources of the period are in that language. It has been said that Americans have a contribution to make in writing European history, since they have perspective and distance from the scene. They can be expected to approach the solution of German historical problems with fewer preconceived ideas than a resident of Munich or Hamburg.

The undergraduate may well ask whether he is potentially qualified to do research on tenth-century Germany or any other topic, and the answer is an emphatic "yes." Although some have argued that even the faculty should not do research and that the dictum "publish-or-perish" has removed the ablest scholars from contact with undergraduates, this has never been proven. It is far more likely (at least in the humanities and social sciences) that those who are the most enthusiastic researchers are also the ablest lecturers. Research and teaching go together in the university, and the one without the other is apt to prove a sterile choice, at least in the long run.

Even those who admit this for the faculty are not so likely to insist on it for graduate students. The Ph.D. program is considered not as a research degree so much as a passport to a teaching job at a small undistinguished college. Advisers seldom expect their degree candidates to publish even a part of their dissertation, and some are even offended if the student himself raises the question. "Research" in many quarters is conveniently passed off as a device for the lazy or an arrogant trick of the empire builders, rather than being recognized for what it is—the *raison d'être* of the university.

Virtually no one suggests that *undergraduates* should attempt research or even be exposed to it. Why? In general, undergraduates have been treated like children who go to the university in much the same way a rich nineteenth-century girl went to a finishing school in Switzerland. There, under the chaperones called professors, they are meant to go to class, write out their homework, and keep their mouths shut. After four years of this deadening activity, they are considered "safe" to enter society and take over their parents' values as well as the family business. Most faculty members worth anything have not concurred in this interpretation of their role, and more and more students are demonstrating (literally as well as figuratively) that they are not children to be herded through school without finding out what higher education is all about.

Assuming, then, that the real purpose of any university worth the name is not to inculcate old values but to seek the truth, however unpopular it may be, the true job of both faculty and students at all levels is to do research in the broadest sense. Whether the results are ultimately published is somewhat irrelevant, for this will usually depend on the quality of the work. Invariably, more senior faculty are going to publish significant articles in a given year than the freshmen. But whatever their stage of development, they should all be doing the same thing—looking for the truth on important topics that appeal to them personally. Maybe tenth-century Germany is such a topic for you. Or maybe there is something else that you are more interested in.

What is the result of the university's encouraging research at all levels? Academic greatness. This was the result at Paris in the twelfth century with public debates on theological topics. This has been the result at Oxford where the tutor meets the student once a week to criticize the paper worked up in the preceding seven days. Debate, tutorial, lecture, and publication can all be considered forms of teaching, and they can also be considered forms of research. Only the media are different.

What is the result for the undergraduate exposed to this kind of teaching? First, he takes his studies more seriously—at least those that appeal to him—instead of rummaging among the offerings of a "free" or "unincorporated" university for a course that seems truly relevant and satisfying. It is only the interested and committed faculty member who can make the field exciting and, if the professor does not believe in the subject enough to investigate its frontiers, the course will be a dull one.

Second, through involvement in a topic concerned with the past, the student will find that there is fallout on problems of present concern. If he becomes engrossed in the question of whether it was "good" for Germany that Otto went to Italy and sought to rule it, he may now transfer this same question to America's involvement in Southeast Asia. Both take research, that is, hard work plus subtle reasoning, to understand. Conversely, students who have already been involved in current problems may find that they can transfer their political acumen back into time to solve a problem of tenth-century historiography.

It works both ways, and there is no end to the intellectual reverberations that such an approach can have. Whether the student ultimately becomes a professor of history is meaningless. He may only sharpen his critical faculties in order to enhance his position as an informed citizen, but this is perhaps the most important position of all.

# SUGGESTED READINGS

Brooke, Christopher, *Europe in the Central Middle Ages, 962–1154* (New York: Holt, Rinehart & Winston, Inc., 1963).

Brundage, James A, "Widukind of Corvey and the 'Non-Roman' Imperial Idea," *Medieval Studies*, XXII (1960), pp. 15–26.

Bryce, James, *The Holy Roman Empire* (New York: Schocken Books, Inc., 1961).

Butler, Mary Marguerite, *Hrotsvitha: The Theatricality of Her Plays* (New York: Philosophical Library, 1960).

*Cambridge Medieval History*, Vol. III, planned by J. B. Bury (Cambridge: University Press, 1922).

Cames, Gerard, *Byzance et la peinture Romane de Germanie* (Paris: Editions A. et J. Picard, 1966).

Duchesne, L., *The Beginning of the Temporal Sovereignty of the Popes, A.D. 754–1073* (London: Kegan Paul, Trench, Trubner, & Co. Ltd., 1908).

Duckett, Eleanor, *Death and Life in the Tenth Century* (Ann Arbor: The University of Michigan Press, 1967).

Folz, Robert, *L'idée d'Empire en Occident du $V^e$ au $XIV^e$ siècle* (Paris: Aubier, 1953).

Gregorovius, Ferdinand, *History of the City of Rome in the Middle Ages*, 4 vols., trans. Annie Hamilton (London: George Bell & Sons, 1894–1896).

Grodecki, Louis, *L'Architecture Ottonienne*, (Paris: Armand Colin, 1958).

Haight, Anne Lyon (ed.), *Hroswitha of Grandersheim: Her Life, Times, and Works, and a Comprehensive Bibliography* (New York: The Hroswitha Club, 1965).

Herzstein, Robert E., *The Holy Roman Empire in the Middle Ages* (Boston: D. C. Heath and Company, 1966).

Kern, Fritz, *Kingship and Law in the Middle Ages*, trans. S. B. Chrimes (New York: Frederick A. Praeger, 1956).

Loyn, Henry Royston, "The Imperial Style of the Tenth Century Anglo-Saxon Kings," *History*, XL (1955), pp. 111–115.

Paetow, Louis John, *A Guide to the Study of Medieval History* (New York: Kraus Reprint Corporation, 1964), copyright 1959, Appleton-Century-Crofts, Inc.

Pullan, Brian, *Sources for the History of Medieval Europe from the Mid-eighth to the Mid-thirteenth Century* (Oxford: Basil Blackwell, 1966).

Schramm, Percy E., *Herrschaftszeichen und Staatssymbolik*, 3 vols. (Stuttgart: Anton Hiersemann, 1954-1963).

Schramm, Percy E., and Florentine Mütherich, *Denkmale der deutschen Könige und Kaiser* (Munich: Prestel Verlag, 1962).

Thompson, James Westfall, *Feudal Germany*, 2 vols. (New York: Frederick Ungar Publishing Company, 1962), copyright 1928.

Ullmann, Walter, "Reflections on the Medieval Empire," *Transactions of the Royal Historical Society*, XIV (1964), pp. 89-108.

White, Lynn, Jr., *Medieval Technology and Social Change* (Oxford: University Press, 1964).

DD
136
.H5

DD
136
.H5